WHERE GOD LIVES

Parmesh Sadan

ATUL JOHARI | SHALINI JOHARI

LAUNCHPAD

An imprint of
Srishti Publishers & Distributors

Srishti Publishers & Distributors
A unit of AJR Publishing LLP
212A, Peacock Lane
Shahpur Jat, New Delhi – 110 049

editorial@srishtipublishers.com

First Published by Srishti Publishers & Distributors in 2026

10 9 8 7 6 5 4 3 2 1

This is a work of non-fiction, based on the author's life. Some events have been fictionalised for dramatic effect. While due care has been taken to verify all information at press time, any inadvertent miss brought to notice shall be updated in the subsequent editions. The views expressed in the book are the author's own and are not intended to hurt the sentiments of any individual, community, sect, group, or religion.

To our Family, without whom all of this would have been impossible...

CONTENTS

PART 1
THE GIRL

1. THE STORY

Back in 2004, we were on a three-month trip to India from Melbourne after migrating to Australia. After dinner, everyone retreated to their rooms—either to get ready for bed or to settle in for a good, long gossip session. But Papa Ji and I had different plans. We were keen to document as much knowledge as possible during those quiet evenings.

My father-in-law, Ravindra Kumar, was on a deeply spiritual journey. Through his meditations, he had visualised a unique version of the Ramayan—one that was truly special. I was determined to preserve it, so I set up my camcorder on a tripod, ready to record.

"When you are ready, Papa Ji, let us begin," I gently prompted. "Tonight, I want to capture the Ramayan as Lord Krishna shared it with you."

After a moment of thoughtful silence, Papa Ji began:

"With the grace of my Guru Lord Sri Krishna, I became aware of this true story. In the process, I also came across various testimonies. This story was first narrated by Ravan's stepbrother Kuber and is still acknowledged in parts of Tibet.

About 1.75 million years ago, Brahma, Vishnu, and Mahesh (Shiva) entrusted Daksha with a monumental responsibility: he was appointed the *Lokpati,* the steward of planet Earth. The mission was to bring together all cultures under a unifying vision of humanity, thus creating what was called the *Vashvik Rajya*—a global kingdom.

The guiding principle of this kingdom was simple: it was all about *giving*, not taking. The focus was to be on what each person could contribute to others rather than what they could gain. This was not about establishing a new religion but embracing a way of life that was rooted in mutual respect, tolerance, and shared humanity. Everyone was to treat each other as part of an extended family. At its heart there was the profound belief that we are all part of *one big family— Vasudhaiva Kutumbakam.*

Shiva, Vishnu, and Brahma were the supreme rulers of the universe, with Earth being one of the many planets under their domain. Their interactions with the people of the Earth occasionally led to the birth of extraordinary offsprings. Some of these children became remarkable figures in their own right, thereby leaving behind a lasting legacy. For instance, Daksha, the son of Brahma, was known for his wisdom and leadership. Shiva's sons, Kartikeya and Ganesh, became iconic figures who were celebrated for their bravery and intellect. Similarly, Vaivats Manu, the son of Vishnu, was celebrated as the originator of humanity, thus playing a pivotal role in shaping civilisation.

Under Daksha's guidance, seven renowned Vasus, popularly known as the *Saptarishis*, were appointed to spread this philosophy across seven distinct regions. These Sages were entrusted with the noble task of teaching and upholding the principles of giving and harmony. The rulers of these regions were chosen for their exceptional character and qualifications. They were honoured with the title of *Dev*, which signifies "those who give". Each Dev embodied this principle in their responsibilities. For example, Indra Dev brings prosperity by ensuring sufficient rain, while Surya Dev provides energy that sustains all life. The followers of this philosophy were called *Arya*, representing those who embraced the path of righteousness and selflessness. The ultimate vision was for the entire world to become an *Arya Samaj* — a united, harmonious society that was built on the values of giving, mutual respect, and shared humanity.

When some Devs began acting against the fundamental philosophy of giving and started focusing on possession and personal gain, they were outcast by the Dev community. This new way of thinking was given a name: *Droh Nav*. *Droh* means to oppose, and *Nav* signifies new. Over time, these individuals came to be known as *Danav*. As the years went by, the Danavs grew stronger, hence posing a significant threat to the Devs. The clashes between the two groups became frequent, which were often centred around resources. One of the most famous conflicts was the *Samudra Manthan*—the churning of the ocean for resources.

Eventually, some individuals from the two opposing sects began to form bonds. From one such union came Ravan. His father, Vishrava, was of divine descent, a son of a Dev, while his mother,

Kaikesi, belonged to the Danava lineage. This unique parentage made Ravan a remarkable individual—wise, knowledgeable, and incredibly powerful.

Recognising Ravan's unparalleled abilities, Lord Shiva believed that he could bridge the divide between the Devs and the Danavs. Ravan was given the title of *Rakshak*, meaning protector, and was made the King of Lanka—the most prosperous and strategically significant land at that time, which was previously ruled by his stepbrother Kuber. Due to this, Kuber relocated his kingdom to Alkapuri, leaving Lanka under Ravan's rule.

Ravan's mission was to maintain balance and prevent war by ensuring that neither the Devs nor the Danavs gain overwhelming power. Around this time, another mighty king emerged—Dashrath—whose stature was similar to Lokpati Daksha. While Ravan was focused on establishing peace in the regions surrounding Lanka, Dashrath was fighting battles to restore order in other troubled parts of the kingdom.

During one of these battles against Ravan, Dashrath was seriously injured but was saved by his second wife, Kaikeyi. Not only was Kaikeyi a skilled warrior, but she was also Ravan's cousin. Kaikeyi's father, Rishi Agastya, and Ravan's father, Vishrava, were both sons of Rishi Pulatsya, the ruler of the region which is now known as Russia. Dashrath had four sons: Ram, born to his first wife, Kaushalya; Bharat, born to Kaikeyi; and the twins Lakshman and Shatrughan, born to his third wife, Sumitra.

Meanwhile, Bali, a powerful yet moderate Danav king, caught Ravan's attention. Hoping to form closer ties, Ravan spent six months with Bali, learning various skills. While some accounts suggest that Ravan attacked Bali and ended up imprisoned during this time, others believe that the two kings forged a bond. During his stay, Ravan married Trizata, the royal dancer at Bali's palace, and eventually returned to Lanka with her. Trizata gave birth to a beautiful daughter, but her birth chart foretold that she would bring destruction to Ravan's kingdom. Troubled by this prophecy, Ravan initially decided to kill the child. However, her exceptional charm softened his resolve, and instead, he abandoned her in a faraway place. She was discovered and adopted by King Janak, who named her Sita.

As Sita grew up, King Janak noticed something extraordinary about her. She possessed incredible strength and could easily lift Shiva's *Dhanush*—a powerful artefact and the last nuclear weapon that was left on Earth by Shiva. Ordinary people could not even push it. This extraordinary ability inspired Janak to devise a unique way to find a suitable match for her. Despite years of love and care, Sita remained a mystery to Janak. He announced that she would marry the one who could lift and use Shiva's Dhanush. This competition, known as Sita's *Swayamvar*, attracted kings and warriors from far and wide, including Ravan and Ram, the eldest son of Dashrath, who was accompanied by his brother Lakshman.

By this time, Ravan had mastered the knowledge of creating nuclear warheads, a skill he had acquired from Shiva himself when he was given the title of *Rakshak*. The land of Lanka was rich in radioactive materials, thus providing the raw elements for these powerful weapons.

At the *Swayamvar*, Sita's introduction captivated everyone. As part of the ceremony, Janak shared how he had found her and revealed that she was his adopted daughter. When Ravan heard this, he realised that Sita was none other than his own abandoned child. Understanding the gravity of the situation and wanting to avoid revealing his connection to her, Ravan respectfully bowed out of the competition, citing his respect for Shiva and the sacred *Dhanush*.

One by one, the other kings tried their strength but failed to even move the *Dhanush*. As Janak grew increasingly anxious, Vishwamitra, the great Rishi who had brought Ram and Lakshman to the event, encouraged Ram to try it. When Ram stepped forward and lifted the Dhanush, the crowd was awestruck. However, as he attempted to string it, the Dhanush broke into two with a thunderous explosion.

The sound brought Rishi Parashuram, who had originally entrusted the *Dhanush* to Janak, rushing to the scene. Furious at first, Parashuram quickly grasped the gravity of the situation and the divine nature of Ram's role. Understanding that Ram and Sita were destined to be together, Parashuram calmed down, blessed the newlywed couple, and returned to his abode, leaving a sense of awe and wonder at what had just unfolded.

Ram, Lakshman, along with Sita came back to Ayodhya. Dashrath, who was now old and frail, decided to retire and make Ram the King. This was not the best outcome for Kaikeyi, who was contemplating the throne for her son Bharat, who had spent most of his time battling his neighbouring rulers. Kaikeyi had full support from her cousin brother, Ravan, and relied on him in case things got out of hand.

Kaikeyi informed Ravan about Dashrath's intentions but was disappointed as Ravan was now more interested in Sita being the queen of the Vashvik Rajya. Kaikeyi had no choice but to turn to her husband Dashrath. She reminded Dashrath about the day she had saved his life and how he owed his life to her. She demanded the throne in favour of Bharat and 14 years of exile for Ram. This would allow enough time for Bharat to establish himself as the preferred king. Dashrath fulfilled her demand and paid back the life he owed to his beloved wife.

When Bharat returned to Ayodhya from war, he did not like the idea of being the king which his mother had planned for him. The death of his father filled him with guilt. He tried to fix the situation by persuading Ram to return from exile and become the king. Ram showed his helplessness. He was tied with his father's last wish. Finally, Bharat agreed to rule the kingdom on Ram's behalf until his return from exile after 14 years.

As per tradition, after Dashrath's death, his three wives left the palace to spend a simple life away from the main town. Overall, this development did not matter much to Ravan. He knew it was just a matter of time before his daughter became the queen. Ram also took this as an opportunity to enhance and test his skills in the real world. He explored the most treacherous parts of the world and became aware of various social dilemmas.

Everything was fine until Ram entered the region that was under the direct control of Srupnakha, Ravan's sister. Ravan had appointed Srupnakha as the governor of this area after killing the chief of the territory, who was in love with his sister but Ravan did not consider him worthy enough for her. When Srupnakha spotted Ram, Lakshman, and Sita in her area, she started monitoring them closely. She discovered all the details about them and became keenly interested in Lakshman. She used every opportunity to contact Lakshman alone and expressed her desire to marry him. Ram had some reservations about formalising the relationship into marriage. Srupnakha took this as an insult. Some books have mocked this instance as if Lakshman had physically cut her nose.

Srupnakha sought the help of her cousin brothers Khar and Dushan. They were the sons of her mother's brother, Marichi. The two did not handle the situation very well and tried to use force on Ram. They underestimated Ram and were killed in the scuffle. Srupnakha took up this matter with Ravan, but she was disappointed since he was reluctant to take revenge.

She wondered, why he was not interested in a relationship that would give him so much political advantage? If her previous lover was not a good match due to being the chief of just a small state, what was wrong with the prince of the whole world? She knew something was not right. She was already perplexed by the uncanny resemblance Sita had with her brother Ravan and his first wife, Trizata. Could she be their daughter? Was this why Ravan avoided marrying Sita?

Srupnakha did not want to be disappointed twice and took a surprising step. She threatened Ravan that if he would not help her, she will reveal that Sita was his daughter. How could his daughter be acceptable for Ram, but his sister was not justified for Lakshman? Either he had to accept both relations or none.

Ravan was not left with much choice. The demand by Kaikeyi to make Bharat the King of Ayodhya in place of Ram had soured the relationship between the two families. The revelation of Sita's secret would further become a recipe for disaster. He thought that if Sita could be persuaded to leave Ram, he could kill Ram and take over Ayodhya. If Lakshman still refused to marry Srupnakha, he would kill him as well. This would unify planet Earth into one kingdom and fulfil his goal.

To implement his plan, he needed approval from Sita in complete secrecy. He made a master plan with the help of Marichi who distracted Ram and Lakshman and took them far away for which he paid the price with his life.

In the meantime, Ravan arrived and opened his heart to his lost daughter but failed to convince her. Ravan needed more time and evidence to prove his point and thus he forcefully took Sita to Lanka. In Lanka, Sita was kept in a tightly secured, confined place where she was united with her mother, Trizata. Despite his best efforts, Ravan still could not convince Sita to leave Ram. Trizata also did not show any significant result. Ravan was aware of Ram's increasing strength.

It did not take long for Ram to establish that Sita was under Ravan's custody. Ram was becoming very popular due to his humble nature, enormous strength, and wisdom. Many displaced warriors who had taken refuge in the jungles were establishing alliances with him. Sugriv was one of them. His brother Bali had kicked him out and had forcefully kept his wife.

Ram killed Bali with the help of Sugriv and Hanuman. Sugriv got back more than his share. This was the turning point, as Ravan lost one of his biggest allies, and Ram now had the support of a vast army. Ram still needed nuclear weapons to match the might of Ravan, a bridge for his army, and artillery to cross the narrow section of the sea that separated Lanka from their approach.

Ram sent Hanuman to Kailash to visit his father, Shiva, to learn about nuclear weapons. At Kailash, Hanuman visited the Shiva Linga, a dome-shaped architecture that was characteristic of all nuclear power stations worldwide. Hanuman created a miniature model of it to help Ram create a Shiva Linga, or a nuclear power station, at Rameshwaram, which is a Holy Place for Hindus even today. Simultaneously, the preparation for building the bridge was gathering pace.

The time was apt to send a clear message to Ravan and collect as much intelligence as possible to fine-tune the preparations. The possibility of striking a deal to avoid war was also high on the agenda. Once again, Hanuman was chosen for the job. Hanuman could run fast enough without breaking the water's surface, like a genus lizard crossing rivers. He was also a great swimmer and had the strength and stamina to cross this patch of sea. He could dodge any attack from the sea creatures or air strikes. He could climb with speed on straight walls. He did not need any weapons. He himself was the biggest weapon. If there was one person who could cross all barriers barehanded, who needed no weapon to demolish an army, and confuse anyone with his wisdom and logic, it was Hanuman. He was perfectly suited for being a messenger who was not allowed to carry any weapon.

Hanuman took the wedding ring from Ram before setting off for Lanka. It was a challenging journey. Once again, some books have provided an oversimplified version of the close encounters that he faced while crossing the sea in the form of a duel with Sursa, who swallowed Hanuman, but he came out of her nostril. After entering Lanka, he found the strategic places, which included Ashok *Vatika,* where Sita was imprisoned. Coincidently, when Hanuman was in Lanka, Ravan visited Sita.

The conversation between Ravan and Sita revealed the secret relationship of them being father and daughter. Later on, Sita confirmed her relationship with Ravan to Hanuman. She asked Hanuman to tell Ram to hurry and rescue her, as Ravan planned to kill Ram to marry her off to someone else. Her plight fuelled Hanuman. He planned to gain time by creating confusion in Lanka by casting doubt on Ravan's victory.

Hanuman, disguised so far, came out in the open and started damaging the nearby fruit trees. This was enough to alarm the guards about a suspected intruder. Due to fear and anxiety, they attacked Hanuman. He quickly acted in self-defence, hurting most of them badly, but intentionally did not kill anyone and left a few so they could escape. A bigger and more advanced battalion joined the battle, but it ended with the same consequences. So far, there had only been a few casualties, but they were enough for high-rankers to take action.

Meghnath, son of Ravan, was next to none on the battlefield. He had won the title of *Indrajit* after defeating Indra, the king of

Devs. He captured Hanuman and brought him to the court of Ravan for interrogation. Hanuman denied all the allegations. He blamed Ravan's army for attacking an unarmed person without any warning or even trying to find the reason for his presence.

Hanuman introduced himself as Ram's messenger. He conveyed Ram's message to let Sita go or be ready to face Ram's fury. Ram would wipe out the whole of Lanka. Further, when Hanuman was about to drop the bombshell about Ravan's secret relationship with Sita in the court, Ravan ordered him to shut up and asked his guards to kill him. Vibhishan, Ravan's younger brother, interfered, and the sentence was reduced to life imprisonment.

As the guards were taking Hanuman to prison, he freed himself. This time, instead of attacking the guards, he spoke politely, "I am not going to hurt any of you. I am not your enemy, and neither is Ram. He is your King. You should pay respect to Ram. He is Ravan's son-in-law. Sita is Ravan's daughter from his first wife, Trizata. She is with her mother in Ashok Vatika. I wanted to ask Ravan why he had captured Sita, but he did not let me speak. He must have ulterior motives. He is putting you all in great trouble. Ravan is your traitor. You all deserve a clarification from him."

This was enough to set a smoke of scepticism in Lanka. Hanuman confused the guards and escaped to join Ram. In Hindi, the tail is called *"Pooch"*. This word has another meaning, "a query". This was Hanuman's query that shook everyone's faith in Lanka, or, in other words, it set fire to Lanka. It had nothing to do with the physical tail or fire.

The damage was done. The battle was already won. Vibhishan was identified as a soft target. The whole army was shocked and demoralised. The people of Lanka were in a fix and deeply divided. Ravan needed time and energy to bring back calm and order in his kingdom. Ram had found a lifetime companion in the form of Hanuman. Both would never separate for the rest of their lives and keep each other close to their hearts.

After constructing the nuclear power station and completing the bridge over the sea, Ram invited Ravan to witness the pilot run of the production of the nuclear warheads. After learning the facts from Hanuman, Ram developed a soft corner for Ravan. He wanted to avoid war. He thought Ravan would back off after inspecting all the preparations and would come to a compromise. Unfortunately, Ravan had already lost everything. He had nothing more to lose apart from his life, which he found unworthy.

The war started, and one by one the great warriors of Ravan's army lost their lives. Vibhishan left Ravan and joined Ram. Meghnath gave a very tough time to Ram's army and almost killed Lakshman, but Hanuman was able to get the medication in time. The very next day, Meghnath was killed by Lakshman. Finally, Ravan succumbed at the hands of Ram. Sita was united with Ram. Vibhishan was handed over the kingdom of Lanka. Ram, along with Lakshman, Sita, and Hanuman, returned to Ayodhya to resume his position as King.

In Ayodhya, Sita's secret did not remain a mystery for long and people started saying all kinds of things about her. Disappointed with the narrow mentality of the people of Ayodhya, Sita left the palace and started living in Rishi Balmiki's *Ashram.* At that time, Sita was pregnant. She gave birth to twins Luv and Kush. Later, Luv and Kush reunited with their father Ram, but Sita refused to return. Ram was disappointed, and he took *Samadhi.* Lakshman followed Ram's footsteps. Hanuman went back to Kailash and started living like a monk. Even now, some people claim to have seen him."

Papa Ji finished the story. His eyes were still lost in deep thought. I quickly checked the quality of the recording and thanked him.

"It is an amazing story. You described the scenes as if you were witnessing everything unfolding before your eyes. I will leave a copy of this for you. You must be tired. I will get you some water."

2. THE FOUNDATION STONE

Since I married Shalu, not a day has passed without a reference to her home, *Parmesh Sadan*, or her hometown, Etah.

Etah is a small district in Utter Pradesh, Northern India. Though it is a stone's throw away from Agra, the city of *Taj Mahal*, and Tundla, a major railway junction, it is not connected by train. This impacts its development; however, since it is connected by GT Road, a major road that connects Northern India, there are some consolations. Etah has earned its name due to its criminal history, mainly due to land disputes. A place that lacks opportunities in proportion to the growing population is a perfect recipe for harvesting crimes. No wonder so many Lawyers and Advocates have made it their home.

Early in 1920, Parmeshwari Dayal was a young teacher in Ajmer (Rajasthan) and found it hard to manage his properties which were spread over the villages of Etah. He decided to move to Etah and started practising Law in the Civil Court. Very soon, he established himself as the top lawyer in the region. He bought a big piece of land offset from GT Road, closer to the heart of the city, to build his residence in typical Jaipur architectural style. This house had 20-foot high ceilings. Artistic pillars supported the central *veranda*. The floor was marble. The house could accommodate cooks, servants, cows, a horse cart, and caretakers. In short, it was like a President's house.

Parmeshwari Dayal was a true professional and a perfect human. By definition, a true professional who worked against his profession by trying to reach the root cause of an issue. A doctor works to eliminate diseases; a teacher aims to eliminate ignorance. This requires courage, passion, leadership, and vision. Parmeshwari Dayal had it all and in plenty. He was the source of light and attraction for all those who wanted to build a healthy and happy society.

Every weekend, Parmeshwari Dayal would have a meeting with his core friend circle. Any visiting dignities and political leaders would be the guests in these conversations to provide fresh perspectives. It became very clear to him that education was a fundamental element for the growth of Etah and was top priority for him.

Parmeshwari Dayal offered a big piece of land for a school, which he had been given as part of fee by one of his clients. This school would provide education from grades six to twelve. The school would have no bias for religion and would aim to produce good human beings. This was just the beginning. The Board of Directors selected by Parmeshwari Dayal from his core group worked extremely hard for the next several years to bring the school to an iconic state. Since its inception, ASA Inter College has not stopped producing great citizens and is still an integral part of the fabric of Etah.

Parmeshwari Dayal had one daughter from his first marriage. The little girl was beautiful but not fortunate, as her mother died when she was very young. From his second wife, Jagrani, Parmeshwari Dayal had four sons and a daughter. Jagrani was a lady of strong character and commanded full respect. She was a great administrator and looked after the home affairs exceptionally well. Jagrani had her cot in the middle of the house, where she would enjoy the full sun and command chefs, servants, and her daughters-in-law.

Jagrani brought Chullu Pandit and Birju along with her in marriage. This was a custom in those days; when a rich family's daughter was married, she would be accompanied by a servant or two from her village to relieve her from the hardships of all the daily domestic chores. Chullu Pandit took charge of the kitchen while Birju looked after all the external matters, that included the two domestic cows. Chullu Pandit and Birju lived in Parmesh Sadan for eleven months a year and took one month off to visit their families.

With time, Parmeshwari Dayal became known as *Mahatma Ji* due to his generosity, simplicity, and charity. He fought for various causes. He did not demand any fee from his clients and accepted anything, even if it was just a blessing. He entertained groups of *Sadhus* and Politicians equally by providing food and accommodation for days in his Parmesh Sadan, the president's house. In his spare time, he enjoyed teaching and playing chess with his grandsons.

Parmeshwari Dayal did not believe in religious rituals. He could only strive to be human, a man with virtues. For this, it was important to have an open mind towards all religions, cultures, and philosophies without becoming attached to the strings that come with any one of them. He wanted to unify all the families, sects, religions, and countries into one society. He became an *Arya Samaji,* where the whole world is the offspring of *Aryans,* the very first Human Race. Maybe many races lived before the Aryans, but they did not rise above the basic needs and were simply a collection of *Homo sapiens.*

"Vasudhaiv Kutumbkam," the whole world is one family, was the Arya Samaj's principle. The family is sustained by contribution, not by possession from everyone. When you give, you get happiness, satisfaction, and peace, that is contrary to possessing, which brings greed, insecurity, and fear. He understood the difference between the wealthy and the rich. Wealth can generate what is required when it is required and as much as it is required. Money cannot buy you love or make you healthy or respected. He knew he wanted happiness, not joy. Happiness brings a smile and spreads like an aroma. Joy spreads jealousy and gives rise to a rat race in society.

3. THE STORYTELLER

My father-in-law, Ravindra Kumar, was the eldest son of Parmeshwari Dayal and Jagrani. He was tall, dark, and thinly built. He was a true reflection of his father; he was gentle, caring, creative, and spiritual. He carried forward his father's practice and traditions and established himself as a top lawyer in the Civil Court. He fought every case for justice, peace, and harmony. He became famous as Lalla Babu in society.

The journey of Lalla Babu from his house to the court was a true transformation of a humble man into a commanding leader. On his way, greetings from all around never stopped. During his arguments in the court, he was clear, forceful, ferocious, and authentic, thus leaving no choice to the judges or his opponent's lawyers by providing references from exact page numbers, journal numbers, the wordings, and the verdict. He demonstrated exceptional memory and professionalism.

When dealing with divorce cases, he tried his best to resolve the differences between the husband and wife. He gave back happiness to the couples, took away their bitterness, and got true blessings from them. At the end of the day, if his wife Saroj asked about his earnings, he smiled cheekily and told her, "Don't ever run after money; it will follow you."

Saroj was an exceptionally beautiful and charming girl. She was tall, slim, and had a very fair complexion. By nature, she was agile, joyful, and caring. Her family was settled in Lucknow. When Saroj was young, education for girls was not a priority at all. If a girl belonged to a wealthy family and wanted to be educated, she would have a teacher visiting at home. Girls were mostly confined to their homes and were skilled by their mothers in areas that were essential for life and to keep the family well looked after.

Essentially, girls were trained in a way that a man could not survive without them. Clearly, at the time, there were two education systems. One that was an informal system, mainly for girls, which created street-smart and worldly-wise people. The other was the formal education system. These two systems complemented each other and kept the overall social structure in a balanced state.

Though there were two complementary education systems, there was only one system for marriage, which was run and governed by the grace of God. It was mainly run through informal networks.

Saroj was no exception; she had hardly finished her high school education when her marriage was settled. She did not know who she was getting married to and what he looked like. Her only information was that her bridegroom was an advocate and that he belonged to a rich and famous family. On the day of the marriage, when the *Baraat* (marriage procession) reached her house and one of her curious relatives saw the bridegroom, she rushed to tell Saroj and her father that this was a complete disaster.

"The boy is no match for Saroj. He is dark, skinny, and has rabbit teeth. If Saroj's mother had been alive, she would not have allowed this to happen."

"I will leave it to you to decide. It is not too late." Saroj's father reassured Saroj.

The stakes were very high and required wisdom, vision, and, above all, care and love to make the right choice and the right choice was made. The celebration prevailed. The grace of God showered on all. Humans are not above God.

At Etah, in Parmesh Sadan, Jagrani kept her daughter-in-law, Saroj, very close to her heart. She appointed a music teacher from Mainpuri, a neighbouring city, to teach vocal music to Saroj. The training went on for three years. Jagrani wanted Saroj to be a good singer like her daughter Shail, who was now married to an IPS Officer and was living away. Jagrani wanted to fill this vacuum.

Ravindra Kumar had learned classical vocal music and *Tabla*. This would make them even better partners. Jagrani encouraged Saroj to read the newspapers and books rather than wasting her time on knitting. She would tell her:

"Why don't you give this to Lakshmi? She can get it done from *Katra Mohalla*. You don't have to torture your eyes."

Saroj read books and newspapers but continued knitting as well. She was good at it and impressed Jagrani with her skills. One winter, Jagrani asked Saroj:

"I liked the flower pattern on the sweater that you made last year for Shail. Can you knit a blouse for me?"

Saroj and Shail respected each other and became good friends. Whenever Shail liked a *Sari*, a typical Indian dress for ladies, she would buy two and gift one to Saroj. Shail and Jagdish, nicknamed Jag, were always given red carpet treatment at their house. Saroj would take full control of the arrangements and ensure that nothing was left to chance. This led Jagrani to have full confidence in Saroj, and she expressed it by handing over the home keys to her. There was a gap of about nine years before a second daughter-in-law came into Parmesh Sadan. All these years cemented the relationship between Saroj and Jagrani.

Saroj and Ravindra Kumar now had three children: Pradeep, Sharad, and Shalini. While Pradeep and Sharad had only one nickname each, Raju and Munnu, Shalini had a unique nickname from her three uncles living in Parmesh Sadan. Ravindra Kumar, her father, called her Lalli; the elder uncle Ashwani, nicknamed Illa, called her by her formal name, Shalini; the middle uncle Suresh, nicknamed Manna, called her Moti (chubby); and the youngest uncle Chadra, nicknamed Bhaiya, called her Kukki. Saroj often called her daughter by the abbreviated name Shalu. All three kids got undivided love from their bachelor uncles and grandparents.

Raju, the eldest one, got the most care and attention; after all, he would be the king of his generation. No one in the family missed any opportunity to pass on their knowledge and skills to him. Shalu, being the youngest girl, got soaked with the shower of love from everyone.

Parmesh Sadan had the gift of a girl after forty years. At her birth, the royal band of Etah called on uninvited and filled the environment with the most popular songs of the time. Birju, loyal to Jagrani and in charge of external affairs, objected to the band and wanted them to go away.

"Why have you guys come here? This is not an occasion to celebrate. Don't you know this is a girl baby, not a boy?"

"We are here to celebrate. After forty years, Babu ji has been gifted with Lakshmi (the Goddess of Wealth) in this palace. It is such good luck." Reinforced the band leader.

Disappointed by the rejection of his appeal, Birju turned to Jagrani for support and was pleasantly surprised by her response.

"Ask the band leader to continue for two hours and bring him inside. I will reward them dearly. Get sweets from *Ghantagarh* (the main shopping strip). No visitor should go without tasting the sweets. God has blessed us."

Shalu knew she was special. As the princess of the palace, she understood that being a princess meant she could not have an ordinary personality. She needed to be beautiful inside and out. She should be caring and charming, skilled and graceful. She needed to be expressive yet not overly vocal. God had given her large, expressive eyes to see beyond people's skin. While she was approachable, she was not to be taken for granted. All the wealth and love in the world were meant for her, but she had to prove herself worthy of them without a doubt. She understood that every stick has two ends; you cannot pick it up from one end without acknowledging the other.

By now, Shail was blessed with three sons and one daughter. Rajiv (Baboo), Sanjay, and Siddhartha (Babbi). The daughter, Shailja, was nicknamed Rani (the queen).

The families of Ravindra Kumar and Shail were a perfect match, using every opportunity during holidays to strengthen their bond. The children of the two families underwent very different upbringings. Raju, Munnu, and Shalini lived in Parmesh Sadan and gained virtues from being in a joint family.

Saroj, being the chief administrator, hardly had any time for her children. Ravindra Kumar dedicated most of his time to his clients. His days were spent in court, evenings at his home office filled with clients, and nights reading law journals to stay updated on the latest judgments and high-profile cases. Occasionally, Saroj teased Ravindra Kumar by asking about Raju's or Munnu's grades and inquiring about how old Shalu was. She frequently reminded him to take a break and focus on family matters:

"You don't have time for home affairs. You need to start thinking about Shalu's marriage. Don't you know girls grow very fast? I want her husband to have a government job. At least he will have regular income and fixed job timings."

"Why do we need to worry about Shalu? She is in good hands with her grandparents. Anyway, girls bring their fate and good luck from God. Our daughter is special. Since we were blessed with her, my practice has expanded. How are Raju and Munnu doing? What is their routine?" Ravindra Kumar would ask.

"Raju is doing well in his studies. He always gets first position in every exam. His English is excellent, and he enjoys reading English newspapers. Sometimes, he updates me with headlines or interesting articles. Your Babu Ji (Father) likes to spend time with him and teaches him English, Maths, and Chess. Last month, he got an award in the district chess championship in his age group.

Babu Ji also calls Munnu when spending time with Raju, but he is shy. Munnu is very caring and always looks after Shalu. The kids are very eager to visit Shail this summer vacation. This time I will also go with them. The whole environment is very different. Jag is always posted at important regions, and there is much to watch, shop for, and enjoy," Saroj replied.

"I agree. You deserve a break too. It is quite hectic for you here."

Ravindra Kumar was interrupted by Saroj's snoring. His face was filled with happiness, calmness, and satisfaction. He murmured, "You get exhausted." Gently, he touched Saroj's forehead and spoke softly, "I love you; God bless you." Saroj changed her posture by turning to the other side, saying, "Love you too, sleep well, you must be tired as well," and she started snoring again.

Ravindra Kumar shared a broad vision which was similar to that of his father's, Parmeshwari Dayal. Recognizing the gap in education for younger children, since ASA Inter College offered grades six to twelve, he decided to establish a primary school called Mayadevi. His sons, Raju and Munnu, were among the first few students to enrol in this school. However, Ravindra Kumar felt he could provide even more to the younger generation. He believed that nothing could be a better gift than music. He contacted a music teacher in Vanasthali Jaipur to fulfil this vision. He offered him the opportunity to relocate to Etah with his family to run a music school.

Ravindra Kumar constructed a three-room house in the Parmesh Sadan campus, where his family of five—parents and their three daughters—could live in two rooms, using the third for music classes. The teacher accepted the offer. Though the music teacher was talented, his teaching style was not the best. He was very strict and did not treat students respectfully, thus limiting the school's potential to expand beyond a few private tuition sessions.

Tragically, within a year or two, the teacher and one of his younger daughters passed away. Another daughter chose to move back to Rajasthan with her mother. However, Vimla, the eldest daughter, decided to remain in Etah since she had no formal education apart from the classical Indian vocal training and Sitar lessons which she had received from her father.

Vimla was talented but shared her father's temper. She was shifted to a smaller room on the first floor of Parmesh Sadan, which was used for keeping bedding and cots during the summer nights. This was where Shalu received her unofficial training in Sitar. This training enabled her to gain direct entry into the Bachelor of Music program at Dayalbagh College in Agra, which was well-known for its music faculty, without needing any prior qualifications. After completing her bachelor's degree and due to her exceptional skill and unique style of playing the Sitar, Shalu was offered a lectureship to teach Sitar to the Higher Secondary students at Dayalbagh College.

4. THE FAMILY AND FUN

Shalu's arrival brought good fortune to Parmesh Sadan. Her elder uncle, Illa, was set to remarry that year. They chose Raj, a local girl but from a different caste, hoping for a fresh start and a happier union. She belonged to a Punjabi business family. Raj was a well-educated teacher. She brought a very different flavour to Parmeshwari Dayal's family. It was a bit challenging for Jagrani, the head of the family.

Manna, the second uncle, was also set to marry that year. He worked at a bank and was the most sociable member of Parmeshwari Dayal's family. Let me tell you a story about the birth of Uncle Manna. Jagrani was fond of jewels. She had a collection of precious stones but did not have *Lal* (Red Coral gemstones). She strongly believed in one of the saints who used to visit their family. Once, when this saint obliged her by granting one wish, she happily demanded a Lal. "Granted", the saint said and left after staying in their hospitality for another few days.

Two years later, when this saint revisited, Jagrani complained to him that she was still waiting for the Lal that he had granted her. The saint replied, "Were you not blessed with a boy the same year? I had to get him, especially for you, from the Mother Goddess. She had given him only for you." In Hindi, Lal also means a son. Thus, Manna was a gift from the Goddess.

Manna uncle got married to Suman. Coming from a big family, she was aware of the traps and twists that life offers and how to navigate them with limited resources. Suman proved herself a good ally of Saroj and covered her when there was a spillover. She encouraged Saroj to stay grounded and not let her emotions get the better of her. After all, people are always ready to take advantage of kind-hearted individuals.

Bhaiya uncle, the youngest one, was the tallest in the family. He was a teacher and a favourite with all the children. He used to take all the children to movies, exhibitions, or the circus and treat them with sweets. At times, Bhaiya requested Saroj to get a proposal for his marriage to her cousin sister, Bina, who was almost equally attractive as Saroj. Bhaiya got married to Bina, but not the cousin sister of Saroj but her niece. The couple resembled Amitabh Bachchan and Jaya Bhaduri, a famous Bollywood couple. Bina was the most educated in the family. She had completed a Master's degree in Science.

Parmesh Sadan had plenty of private space for every family member and a large common family area. However, the family was growing. Shalu now had a sibling and cousins, thus there was plenty of company and grounds to develop new skills. She did not have the undivided attention of her uncles any more, as they now had children of their own. The priorities were changing, and the focus shifted to their unit families. Still, it was a lot of fun. There was one central kitchen, which now catered to eighteen family members. Jagrani had assigned some tasks to her daughters-in-law to help Chullu Pandit, the chef. Apart from this, each lady was responsible for catering to their children's special needs.

Due to the age differences, children had different dietary requirements, and no one other than their mother could serve it better. All the family members were served food together. Kids brought their allocated steel plates and tumblers with their names inscribed on them. The steam and aroma from hot food, the excitement of all the children, the warmth of the elders, the charm of all the house ladies, and the perfection of chef Chullu Pandit created an atmosphere of an orchestra that would spellbind any guest who witnessed this everyday food festival.

Today, Bina, Saroj's cousin sister, was the guest. Bhaiya uncle was at his best behaviour. He had worn his best clothing and had a good shower in the morning. He was standing close to Saroj, expecting Bina to join them for a chat. Not long after, Bina joined the two, and started expressing her feelings in an awestruck manner. She had never witnessed such a large, happy family with so much fun going on every day.

Bhaiya uncle was not listening but was just watching her until Bina finished with a comment, "I wish I would have been a daughter-in-law in this house like you, Didi." Bhaiya uncle echoed without realising, "I wish." The two locked eyes for a moment and blushed, then they both rushed to take their spot for the meal.

****

The festival of colours, Holi, was just a week away, and preparations were in full swing. Among all the festive dishes, the irresistible *Gujia* took centre stage. The veranda buzzed with activity as the women of the house gathered to work their magic. The dough, made of fine flour, was ready, and the delicious stuffing of milk-cake had already passed the taste test—courtesy the kids, of course!

Next up, small portions of the dough were shaped into neat balls, then rolled out thin and circular, like *chapatis*. Saroj and Suman handled this task expertly, and then swiftly passed each rolled-out piece to Bina and Raj. Their job? Place the milk-cake filling in the centre, fold the dough into a perfect semicircle, and seal the edges using a smart tool—a spoon-like device with a small, toothed wheel on the other end. It trimmed and sealed the Gujias in one smooth motion.

One of the bigger rooms had been cleared out for the next step. Neatly covered with fine white cloth, four cots were ready to keep the raw Gujias. Layered delicately and covered with another white cotton sheet, the Gujias were left to "rest" before their golden moment: deep frying. The frying stage was a delicate process. The timing was everything—you could not afford gaps between frying batches, nor could the raw Gujias sit for too long, as they would dry out and crack while frying, thus spoiling the ghee. A perfectly synchronised effort was required—no project manager needed, just teamwork and experience!

Amidst all this, Shalu decided to take a break from the game of seven tiles that she had been playing with her cousins. With a sparkle in her eyes, she jumped over to lend a helping hand to her mother. Holi was not just about colours but also about togetherness, traditions, and the joy of creating memories.

"I want to make these small balls."

"Look at your hands. Go and clean them properly first."

Replied Suman Aunty.

Shalu rushed away and returned immediately in case anyone changed their minds.

"Here I am." Announced Shalu, squeezing herself in, plucking a portion of the dough, and rolling it in her palm. In no time, the pure white dough ball turned grey. Bhaiya uncle, who was standing nearby, noticed and commented:

"Kukki, you are shedding your colour."

"Maa! Stop Bhaiya uncle, he is teasing me. This is no good. I am going back to play".

All the ladies smiled and continued their work. They needed to cook at least five hundred Gujias.

Illa uncle, who was watching it, took charge:

"Bhaiya, you wait for your turn. We will soak you with all the colours, so you cannot escape from having a shower this Holi. This is the one day in the year when you take a shower, and you try to ditch that as well."

On the other side of the veranda, Manna uncle was sitting on a low cot in shorts and a singlet. He was preparing to polish all his five pairs of shoes. Both Illa and Manna uncle were very particular about dressing up. They ensured that they always look impressive and have the right fragrance. Shalu also liked dressing up elegantly and would wonder why her dad could only be seen in his black suit, a conventional attire for lawyers, or very loose-fitting white *Kurta-Pyjamas*. Once, she had asked him why he didn't dress up smartly like his two brothers and had received a reply with a gentle smile, "Those who know me, it doesn't matter to them how I dress up, and those who don't know me it doesn't bother me in any way."

However, his wife, Saroj, always ensured that he wore clean and ironed clothing. Manna uncle had hardly started polishing his shoes when Illa and Bhaiya approached him with their pair of shoes. Next to them was Shalu, standing with her little pair of shoes. "Manna uncle, can I leave this with you as well? I will pluck your forty grey hairs at no cost today". As a routine, Manna uncle gave a pack of Poppins, a favourite lolly of the time, to every kid who plucked forty grey hairs from his head, as each pack of Poppins cost forty paise. So, one paisa for every grey hair.

Tonight, the Holi Fire would be lit. Everyone was on high alert. No furniture was to be left outside, as the boys on the street would pick it up and put it into the pile of wood that was collected near major road crossings. All these would be burnt in the name of *Holika Dahan* (The Holy fire which consumed the evil lady who tried to burn Prahlad, a devotee of God Vishnu. Instead, she was burned herself, even though she was believed to be immune to fire).

The boys on the street closely guarded their woodpile against the other neighbourhood boys. Everyone was after an easy win. Once the fire was burnt, the families in that particular area would come to pay their homage and worship. The Goddess of Fire would purify their souls. However, this ritual was not followed by the family of Parmeshwari Dayal. They were busy preparing the *Tesu* colour for the next day. Tesu is a flower which is also known as *Palash*.

When soaked overnight in water, the Tesu flowers release a stunning golden colour that captures the essence of Holi. However, not everyone uses Tesu flowers to prepare colours traditionally. The process is time-consuming and costly, and with the rise of quick and inexpensive chemical colours, many opt for convenience. Still, for those who cherish tradition, a small portion of Tesu flowers is boiled to produce a rich, longer-lasting golden colour. This special dye is then used to colour the white saris for the women of the house, who are ready to wear them for the evening festivities after the day-long celebration of colours.

As the sun rises the next day, the streets come alive with groups of boys and men who are eager to celebrate Holi. Armed with wet colours and the ever-popular dry *Gulal*, they step out in vibrant teams. Passersby, beware—no one is spared as these cheerful mobs surround you, shouting the iconic phrase, *"Holi Hai, Bura Naa Maano!"* (Don't mind, it's Holi). Young kids, giggling with excitement, launch water-filled balloons from balconies and dart away to avoid capture. Meanwhile, some group members drum on empty canisters with sticks, mimicking a band for their playful "army."

The celebrations extend to every doorstep. The group pauses at nearly every home, and are greeted with sweets, drinks, and hearty smiles. Some households even serve *Thandai,* a festive beverage that might have a hint of *Bhang* (Marijuana) to add a playful twist. Holi is a festival of joy, togetherness, and breaking barriers—where strangers become friends and laughter knows no bounds.

From a distance, Holi's chaos seems overwhelming, even intimidating at times. But the moment you step into the vibrant whirlwind of celebrations, you find that it is pure magic. This festival of colours is not just about fun; it embodies the spirit of life itself. With its unique blend of tradition, excitement, and unity, Holi truly deserves recognition as an international celebration of joy.

It was the morning of the festival of colours, Holi, at Parmesh Sadan. Shalu, along with her young army, was full of energy. They had already put colour on each other, their parents, and their uncles. Bhaiya uncle had gone into hiding, locking himself in a room. This matter was left to be dealt with later by Illa and Manna uncles, who were, at that moment, busy enjoying a few alcoholic drinks and some sweets to build up their strength and stamina for the next four to five hours. Ravindra Kumar was occupied with greeting groups and guests and serving sweets. Raju and Munnu, the elder sons, were helping their father while also colouring the guests.

Soon, Manna and Illa uncles joined the team, and after a couple of hours, they turned their attention to the ladies of the house. They soaked them in various colours, focusing on the dark shades for their faces and hair. This sight somewhat scared Shalu, who went to complain to Jagrani. But on this day, nothing worked—no rules applied, and no hierarchy stood.

After the ladies of the house were tackled, Bhaiya uncle was forced out of his hiding spot and subjected to playful torture for fifteen to twenty minutes. No part of his body was spared from colour. He was then given a mud bath and made to stay until half-dried before being released on the condition that he take a proper shower and ensure that no spot of colour remained on him. If he failed, another mud bath awaited him.

By evening, the fun and chaos of the festival were over. Everyone had bathed and dressed smartly, ready for gossip which was followed by dinner. However, traces of colour still lingered around their ears and palms. Manna uncle was struggling with a hangover from the special Bhang-mixed drinks that he had consumed in excess. Every few minutes, he tilted slightly to one side, as though gravity was pulling harder on his right side, thus making his posture unstable and requiring constant adjustments. Illa Uncle, with his better capacity, thanks to the extra fat around his waist, had coped better, sticking to alcoholic drinks. Yet, his red, tired, and sleepy eyes told a different story. Bhaiya uncle still looked slightly annoyed, clearly with the rough treatment that he had endured earlier.

"Dada, you must tell Illa and Manna to use only dry colours." Bhaiya uncle complained. Ravindra Kumar did not answer but returned a consoling smile.

"Yes, leave these dirty colours for the cheap people. Everyone looks to us for inspiration. If we behave like animals, what can we expect from others?" Jagrani raised her voice.

"Bhabhi, can we have some Gujia while we wait for dinner? I want to sleep early today. I am very tired." Illa uncle changed the topic.

The ladies started moving towards the kitchen to arrange for dinner. Kids were not showing any signs of slowing down and were busy boasting stories about how they managed to colour their uncles and aunties without getting caught.

5. SUNSET

Parmeshwari Dayal's family was undergoing growing pains. The need for decentralisation of control was challenging the benefits of a united family. The pressure had built up for splitting the kitchen to cater to individual family needs. There was an imbalance in the number of children that each family had, so it was getting harder to decide the contribution which each family head needed to make.

To make it worse, this equation had a few more variables. First, the contribution was, to a degree, voluntary. Second, Ravindra Kumar and Illa's income was not fixed, unlike Manna and Bhaiya. Third, Raj worked full-time, so she could not handle the household responsibilities like Saroj, Suman, or Bina. Even the idea of individual modern toilets closer to the bedrooms floated around.

Parmeshwari Dayal had seen all aspects of his life fulfilled and had stopped practising law. He was now looking after only important matters of the ASA Intercollege. Though all his sons were members of the managing committee of ASA Inter College, Illa uncle was keen to become the manager of the committee and take over all the matters of ASA Intercollege as his law practice had not taken off as much as he would have liked.

As per the rule, a school manager could not have a full-time job. This ruled out the nomination of Manna and Bhaiya uncles for being manager. Ravindra Kumar was not keen, as he barely had any spare time. Manna uncle was happy to ally with Illa uncle in most matters. Bhaiya uncle was focused on setting up a private coaching centre in the portion of the house which had earlier been built by Ravindra Kumar for the music college and thus preferred to be passive on this issue.

One fine day, Parmeshwari Dayal called all his sons and declared that he was satisfied with his life and would depart from this physical world once the sun entered the auspicious north cycle. This reminded me of the character Bhisham in the epic *Mahabharat*, who had the blessing of death by wish, and despite being wounded by hundreds of arrows by Arjun, he held his breath till the sun entered the auspicious north cycle. I still wonder if Parmeshwari

Dayal sensed the change of time or if his soul had been pierced by hundreds of arrows that society and his close relatives and family members had given him.

Soon, the day came, and Parmeshwari Dayal got off his chair, put a white bedsheet on the ground, lay down on it, aligned his head north and his legs south, and left peacefully for the next journey. The news of the departure of the great soul spread like wild fire, and hundreds and thousands people from all directions started coming to pay their homage. This continued for weeks. Everyone said, "*Babu Ji was Mahatma* (a great soul)." I see it slightly differently; nobody is born with a great soul; it is a journey that a person takes through their actions and experiences to become human and leaves with the identity of Mahatma (a great soul), deities, or even God.

Before his death, Parmeshwari Dayal had made his will, in which he allocated portions of Parmesh Sadan to his sons. The combined kitchen could not continue for long, and now, there were four units within Parmesh Sadan. The Ladies of the house were somewhat free to steer their unit families in their desired direction.

****

Shalu's elder brother, Raju Dada, had completed his secondary education and moved to Allahabad University for higher education. Raju Dada was admitted to this university due to his exceptional scores in secondary college. On the other hand, Munnu Dada maintained a low profile within Parmesh Sadan and was happy to spend most of his time with his family. Shalu was loved by all the uncles and aunties, and was the central floating member within the four families of Parmesh Sadan.

It was the festival of *Raksha Bandhan*. This festival is celebrated to strengthen the bond between brother and sister. The sister ties an auspicious thread around her brother's forearm, and her brother promises to guard his sister against any threat. This allowed Shalu to establish her supremacy among all her brothers, irrespective of their ages. Guria, her cousin sister, was still young to dominate and was content with the love and care within her family unit, being the only child.

Shalu had lined up all her brothers and demanded that they touch her feet respectfully before she tied the auspicious thread around their arms. Uncles and aunties tried to persuade Shalu, but the eldest cousin brother, Baboo Dada, who was fourteen years older, had happily bowed to the condition. This left no escape for anyone else.

It had been only a few days since the festival of *Raksha Bandhan*. Shalu's elder brothers, Raju Dada and Munnu Dada, had set up a badminton court on the grounds of Parmesh Sadan. Shalu's cousin brothers, the Tingals (Shail *Bua's* family), were regular visitors. Usually, Raju and Babbi Dadas formed a team against Munnu and Sanjay Dadas. The badminton court was open-air, but with the wind calm this season and ample sunlight, the games provided great entertainment for all the older brothers.

Today, Shalu wanted to join the fun and was pushing her luck. Although she had been promised a practice game later, this assurance did not satisfy her. She walked onto the court and started hanging on the net. Despite a warning from Raju Dada, she continued her tricks and did not back down. This was enough to trigger Raju Dada's frustration, and he reached for Shalu and slapped her hard. This response was unexpected. Shalu cried in pain and humiliation.

Seeking comfort, she turned to her parents, who showered her with love and consolation but did not promise any action against Raju Dada. Next, she approached her grandmother, Jagrani, but found that little had changed. Jagrani hugged her tightly, her eyes filled with sympathy. She wiped her own tears first and then wiped Shalu's tears, repeatedly saying, "Raju should not have hit you so hard."

Shalu underestimated Raju Dada's position in Parmesh Sadan. He was the most beloved and was seen as the true successor of the family legacy. While Shalu held onto Jagrani and sobbed, Raju Dada approached her. Gripped by fear, Shalu tightened her hold, anticipating another slap. She was mistaken. Raju Dada knelt beside her, placed a hand on her shoulder, and gently patted her head. He had come to check on Shalu, leaving his game unfinished. They sat together in silence for a while, with no words spoken.

Shalu was in fourth grade when Parmeshwari Dayal passed away. She attended the school where Raj aunty served as the principal. Although there was a Convent school nearby that had a much better educational standard and reputation, Shalu's family believed that this school would provide her with the care and attention which she needed. However, Raj aunty did not acknowledge Shalu's special status; instead, she treated her like any other student, perhaps even more strictly, to avoid perceptions of favouritism towards her niece.

Shalu was performing well in this school as there was little competition. It was an all-girls school, and most students came from nearby villages. One day, Raj aunty slapped Shalu over a disciplinary issue. This behaviour was unacceptable to the other members of Parmesh Sadan, especially Jagrani, the house chief. Jagrani confronted Raj aunty and firmly instructed her to never repeat such behaviour in future.

Vrinda, nicknamed Guria, was ready to go to school. She was admitted to the Convent school instead of the school where her mom was the principal. It was hard for Saroj to comprehend why the logic of care and attention had changed. Why was Shalu not sent to the Convent school? The trend had changed. Most younger kids from Parmesh Sadan would now go to a Convent school for a better and brighter future. Shalu left this school in grade seven and joined GGIC (Government Girls Inter College). Shalu was ready to face tough competition. She had to catch up with lost ground.

Even though the kitchens were now separate, the traditional celebration of family birthdays, especially for children, was still observed with great care. Each celebration began with a religious ceremony where a Holy man would tell stories of God. Afterwards, all the elderly family members would offer their blessings and apply a *Tilak* to the forehead of the birthday child. After these rituals, the entire family would come together to share a meal. While the meal was not extravagant, it possessed the necessary grace and charm to unite the families.

****

Diwali is a major festival in India. This is celebrated to remember the return of Lord Ram to Ayodhya after fourteen years of exile and his win in the great war with Ravan, the king of Lanka. Today, hundreds of *Deeyas* (small earthen shallow bowls) had been soaked in water for a couple of hours and then wiped with cotton cloth before being filled with *Ghee*. Small cotton balls were stretched and rolled into the palm to form about a four-centimetre-long tight thick thread (*Batti*) for each *Deeya*. These *Battis* were soaked in the Ghee to be lit at night to provide light. These little lighted *Deeyas* would be placed in all the rooms and all along the boundary of Parmesh Sadan's roof, about a foot apart.

Every child was responsible for covering a certain area so that Parmesh Sadan would light up with these *Deeyas* in about fifteen minutes to provide a spectacular light show for the next two to three hours. Children's excitement was at its peak. They had completed the task of placing all the lighted *Deeyas* in their respective places. Parmesh Sadan had come into its full glory, yet it could not beat the lightened faces of the kids who were now proudly watching their work and waiting for the firecrackers. The streets were already filled with the sound and smoke of firecrackers. The sky was lightening up from time to time with the sparkles that were shed by the rocket firecrackers.

For elder family members, especially Jagrani, this festival had a unique charm: the game of cards, Flash. This was played with money as stakes, and special guests and all the older family members were allowed to participate. Kids were allowed to participate from the sidelines by betting on who would win the current round and get prize money from the winner if the bet proved right. This rule did not apply to Shalu. She used to get her cut irrespective of whether her bet was right or wrong, though the amount differed and was based on the result. If this was not enough, Shalu would also receive an additional tip for serving tea and snacks during the game. Of course, the tea and snacks were prepared by the ladies of the house, but the privilege of serving was reserved for Shalu.

For the next week or so, the game would continue each night for three to four hours. Jagrani had her special rules and requests enforced in case she had not won a round for some time. This involved exchanging places with the winning player, playing the round with two or four cards instead of the standard three, winning the game by the least significant combination instead of the most significant one, and distributing the cards in reverse order. The game would end soon if all these failed to change her luck.

****

It had been just over five years since the death of Parmeshwari Dayal. Illa uncle was enjoying being the manager of ASA Inter College. The staff of the school engaged his evenings. To get a higher status and have a favourable approach, teachers and staff paid individual visits to share the shortcomings of others. By now, the school had stationed at least two full-time low-ranking staff members to help with household activities for Illa Uncle's family. The rules of the game had changed. Once, Parmeshwari Dayal was pointed out for using a pencil from the school stationery as an unfair practice. Certainly, this had left Jagrani with a sour taste. Therefore, she was finding it hard to navigate the changing environment. Though she could still hold her position, the reach of her command was shrinking.

One morning, after doing her morning routine of brushing and gargling, Jagrani had difficulty in getting up and started falling to one side. Manna uncle rushed to help her, but she could not get up. By now, Bhaiya uncle and the other house ladies had also joined. The resident homoeopathic doctor examined Jagrani. She was confused by the loss of control over her left hand and leg and was crying and shouting with fear. The resident homoeopathic doctor at Parmesh Sadan was one of these people who had retired as a BDO (Block Development Officer) and had found shelter here. Jagrani was helped to get back to her cot. BDO Sir announced that a stroke had paralysed her left body. He was busy consoling Jagrani that with his medicines, she would regain control and be able to use her impacted left hand and even walk with the help of a stick. The next day, the two Etah district doctors visited Jagrani, confirmed the diagnosis, and prescribed the medicines. Jagrani had more faith in homoeopathic medicines and regular care that BDO Sir could provide.

After this episode, Jagrani was restricted to her room and depended on her daughters-in-law's care. Though Bina aunty and Suman aunty sometimes came to rescue Shalu's mother, Jagrani would always call Saroj for help. BDO Sir was regularly spending time with Jagrani, and with his medicines, she could now use her left hand to get some light breeze from her manual fan. Shalu visited Jagrani daily to tell her stories and get her blessings. This lasted for hardly six months when one evening Jagrani became very anxious. She felt that she was surrounded by little insects and wanted Saroj to be around. She could see that her time had come. Jagrani held tightly to Saroj's hand, repeating her name: "*Bahu, Bahu, Bahu.*" *Bahu* means daughter-in-law, and for Jagrani, daughter-in-law only meant Saroj. Raj aunty asked Jagrani to focus her last breaths in the name of Lord Ram, but Jagrani responded in a somewhat annoyed tone:

"*Bahu* has done everything for me. I will call only *Bahu, Bahu, Bahu….*" Her voice kept fading until it stopped completely.

Saroj had lost her mother when she was young. Jagrani had filled that space for her. Now, once again, Saroj was left without a mother. She also had the additional responsibility of keeping the family together as one big family. Jargrani had lived a royal life, and her sons planned a big procession to celebrate her death to allow everyone to pay her a last visit.

The loss of Parmeshwari Dayal was the loss of society and was likely to be filled by another great leader, but the loss of Jagrani was the loss of Parmesh Sadan alone. Would there be anyone again with the authority and determination to hold the family tight and hold the true meaning of Parmesh Sadan? Parmesh means God, and Sadan means House. The House of God. The place where God lives. The place where everyone is loved. The place where everyone belongs and feels secure. The place that has all the ingredients that nature offers which turns a man into a human being and a human being into a God. The place where there is no scarcity and no fear to put others before themselves.

Almost ten months had passed since Jagrani's death. Suman aunty had made all preparations for her trip today to see her parents. Manna uncle was ready to go to his shop. Since he lost his job in the bank, he had opened a shoe shop. When he came to the veranda, he met Ravindra Kumar and stopped to chat.

"Dada, soon it will be a year since Maa's death. She had a good life, and we should celebrate her death anniversary in a big way. Both the older members of the family are gone, and we all are young and have a long time to live. No one is going to die soon. Let us all chalk out a plan tonight." Manna uncle took the initiative.

"Yes, good idea. I will let Bhaiya and Illa know." Ravindra Kumar replied.

"Bye, Dada. See you tonight." Manna uncle was happy to get his elder brother's approval.

Manna uncle arrived at the shop. Bheeru, the shop's helping hand, opened the shop and started brooming.

"I am not feeling quite well." Manna uncle said to the helping hand and lay down on the bench.

When Bheeru finished brooming and reached the bench, he found Manna uncle lying still. He was not breathing. Bheeru raised an alarm, and shopkeepers from the nearby shops arrived. Manna uncle was no more. The news reached Parmesh Sadan. Birju rushed to the bus stand to bring Suman aunty back.

Things changed drastically in half an hour. Manna uncle left his young wife and three little kids behind without any financial backing. Everyone was looking for an answer to this untimely young death in the family. What had that saint said to Jagrani?

"I had to get Lal, especially for you, from Mother Goddess. She gave him only for you." Saroj had heard this story from Jagrani on a few occasions. Saroj held tightly to Suman aunty and consoled her.

6. DAYALBAGH DEGREE COLLEGE AGRA

In another couple of years, Shalu finished her intermediate college with first division and was ready for higher education at the university. Etah had a degree college, almost on the district's outskirts, which had a bad reputation with regard to its education standards. Raju Dada firmly believed that Shalu should leave Etah for higher education. He suggested Banasthali College in Rajasthan. This was an exclusive institution for girls and focused on providing overall personality development. It had facilities for horse riding, swimming, field games, music, dance, debates, plays, and many more activities.

Though Shalu's parents liked the idea but, due to its distance from Etah, they decided in favour of Dayalbagh Degree College in Agra. Girls from Etah were studying in this college and provided positive feedback. What appealed most to Shalu's parents was the reputation of the hostel warden. She was renowned for her strictness and did not allow the girls from her hostel to go loose. At this tender age and with the taste of first freedom, the security and safety of the daughters was of prime concern for their parents.

Shalu wanted to take up instrumental music in Sitar as her preferred subject for a Bachelor of Arts (BA) degree. However, the music faculty did not offer it as a subject to her since she had not studied it at her intermediate college. Shalu did not give up and persuaded Mr Lahri, the Sitar teacher, to take her test. Mr Lahri was convinced after listening to her performance. Vimla Didi had prepared her well. Though she played in a style that was quite different from what Dayalbagh College taught, but it was impressive. It included all the intricacies and flow that Mr Lahri was looking for. He knew then that this girl would bring a new fragrance to Sitar and she had skills to offer, not just to receive.

The ordeal was not yet over for Shalu. The hostel warden had to be convinced to allow her a place in the hostel. As the Etah district had a bad reputation for being a disturbed area due to the influence of dacoits, the warden was extra cautious about admitting girls from Etah. Shail Bua and Saroj went to meet the warden. Shail

Bua was well-versed in dealing with such delicate moments and manoeuvred the warden to agree.

Shail Bua, Saroj, and Shalu were leaving the hostel campus after convincing the warden. Everyone had a smile on their faces, though the expression of the smile on each face was slightly different. Shail Bua had a winning smile. Saroj had a smile that was mixed with sadness and uncertainty. Shalu had a smile which was mixed with adventure and hope. They planned to return to Parmesh Sadan by the evening so had enough time to explore the campus and have some South Indian snacks. The new batch in Dayalbagh College would start in another month and a half.

Dayalbagh is a city which is located at one end of the main Agra district. The entrance comprises an open gate that creates the impression of entering a new place. On the left side of the road are residences, that are primarily occupied by family followers of the Dayalbagh sect. On the right side of the road stands a brick wall that surrounds the college campus and the girls' hostel.

Several gates in the wall provide separate entrances for the hostel and various faculties, which include the Arts Faculty, Science Faculty, and Engineering College. Once you pass through the gate, reaching the respective faculty takes about a quarter to half a kilometre. Behind each faculty, fruit trees have been planted by the school on the available land. The far end of the campus is secured with a fence to prevent outsiders from entering. Additionally, there is a temple on the campus where the chief Guru of the Dayalbagh sect holds assemblies, leads prayers, and conducts functions.

The first three months in the hostel were challenging for Shalu. For the first time in her life, she found herself away from the secure environment of Parmesh Sadan and the love and care of her parents and family. The hostel room was spacious enough to accommodate three single beds and study desks. Shalu shared the room with Anupma and Neeta, who were also from Etah district. The food in the mess was the most challenging aspect for Shalu, who found herself in tears almost every mealtime during those initial months.

The hostel warden was very strict and would visit any time to ensure that everyone was present and that order was maintained.

Non-vegetarian food, including eggs, was not allowed in the hostel. No girl could leave the premises without registering her name in the logbook at the gate. The guard was loyal to the warden. Any attempt to persuade or charm him into bending the rules was futile. The college required the students to wear a standard white uniform, which made it easy to identify them in the city. On Sunday, the girls were permitted to go out for shopping and recreation, but only for a limited time.

Shalu was starting to adapt to the hostel life. Often, she and Anupma teamed up to visit the city to watch movies, enjoy meals at restaurants, and go shopping. On the other hand, Neeta was a studious girl who preferred to stay in the hostel. One day, Shalu brought boiled eggs into the hostel and enjoyed them without realising that someone had informed the warden. Fortunately, by the time the warden arrived, she had disposed of the shells. To eliminate any lingering smell, she had also sprayed a mild perfume.

"What is going on in this room? Who has brought eggs here?" The warden was furious and started looking for the eggs or any remains.

"No one brought eggs here," Shalu replied. She was shaken. This was a close call, and she could immediately be expelled from the hostel for this unreligious act.

"What are these white bits on your bed? Aren't they remains of eggshells?" The warden was trying to corner Shalu. Very little remains of eggshells were still visible on the bed.

"These must be the plaster from the roof. It keeps coming off. The paint is so old and needs a fresh coat. You can check these." Shalu picked a small piece and offered it for inspection, knowing that the warden would not soil her hand with it.

"I do not need any proof. Clean up this mess. This is the last warning. If you ever do this again, the administration will immediately expel you from the hostel. Is that clear?" The warden was staring at Shalu in anticipation of getting a confession. Shalu held her ground firmly as if nothing had happened and this was all just misinformation. The warden left the room. She had done her job. She left everyone scared, which ensured that discipline prevailed. Law and order prevailed.

"Who could it have been?" Shalu murmured and took a deep breath. The risk was not worth it. She could have enjoyed the eggs at the hawker itself.

A new young Sitar teacher, Sudipta Ma'am, joined the faculty and used to stay late in the college to practice music. This was a perfect opportunity for Shalu to practice and improve her Sitar. She could not do this in her hostel room as it disturbed her roommates. She had taken permission from the warden to stay in the college till late to practice the Sitar. Although, Shalu played the Sitar well but she was not the best in her class. Only more practice could lead her to first place.

Shalu was now in her BA final year. She had moved to the hostel for senior students. These hostels were a bunch of three-room units. Every unit had two big rooms to accommodate three students each, and the third room was small enough to accommodate just one student. The unit had its own toilet and bathroom. Luckily, Shalu shared her room with Anupma only, who would not object to her Sitar practice. Shalu and Anupma had been sneaking into the farms behind their hostel to enjoy the free fruits. A few more girls also joined them occasionally. One of them was a chubby girl named Sadhna.

One day, while Shalu and her friends were busy picking oranges, Anupma spotted the farm keeper approaching them. She raised an alarm, and all the girls ran back to their hostel. Sadhna pleaded with them to help her, but Shalu advised her to hide in the nearby bushes while the other girls distracted the keeper. All the girls fled away in a moment, leaving Sadhna to her fate. Half an hour later, Sadhna joined the girls, who were keenly waiting for her.

Sadhna was upset. Though she had escaped the eyes of the keeper, she went through a reality check. There were no real friends out there. Everyone was after fun. Sadhna kept crying and swearing at her friends. Shalu and Anupma stayed with her until she was a little composed, and then they dropped her to her room. It was another close call; the adventure was not worth the risk. Yet the adventure resumed in two weeks, though now it was just the two of them, Shalu and Anupma, in complete secrecy.

Hostel life shaped Shalu's personality in significant ways. Now, she had place for a little devil in her mind, but she kept it firmly under control, never allowing it to overshadow her kindness, care, and generosity. This balance made her unique and creative. Shalu constantly sought to look beyond the ordinary. She had a knack for reading between the lines and could interpret unspoken words. Her ability to select items from shops that others easily overlooked left her peers baffled. They would often return to the market the next day in search of the same thing, only to come back empty-handed.

Recently, Shalu had begun to speak less, but paradoxically, it made more sense when she did. Her clothing choices evolved to include subtle contrasts instead of just plain colours, and her hair was developing soft curls. Her charm now possessed a hint of fear, commanding respect, and affection. Shalu also honed her ability to see things from multiple perspectives, while fully embracing her unique viewpoint.

Only three months remained until the final year of the BA exam. The girls were dedicating more time to their studies, but Shalu and Anupma still enjoyed their free time by exploring the city. Anupma had never been particularly serious about her academic performance and was content with simply completing her degree. In contrast, Shalu possessed an exceptional memory and focus, which allowed her ample time for other activities. While in the city that weekend, Anupma noticed a poster at a busy intersection. It advertised a music concert at the Taj Hotel, a luxurious five-star establishment.

"Did you see that poster about the music concert in Hotel Taj? You may like to watch this show." Anupma pointed towards the poster.

"Wow, Zakir Hussain. I can't miss this show. It is just two weeks away." Shalu screamed.

"Do you know him? He looks so handsome." Anupma commented.

"He is the best Tabla player in the world. Hariprasad Chaurasia and Shiv Kumar Sharma are also performing. They are the number one in Flute and Santoor. How amazing." Shalu was shivering with excitement. Three of the most excellent musicians in one show. This was a lifetime opportunity.

"The tickets must be costly. How will you afford it?" Anupma was a bit worried.

"Maybe Lahri Sir and Sudipta Ma'am can help us. Our music faculty has a good reputation. They must have some clout. If other students of the music faculty are interested, then it will be easy to persuade them. I will take the initiative." Shalu was bubbling with ideas.

Shalu worked hard to get twelve girls interested in the show. The organisers agreed to oblige the music faculty of Dayalbagh College. Shalu, Lahri Sir and Sudipta Ma'am's hard work made it possible. The college also arranged a minibus to pick up all the girls from the hostel and drop them back safely. The show would finish late at night. The warden had ensured the safety and security of all the girls. She could not take any chance. The show was unforgettable. Four hours seemed like four minutes. It was absolute perfection which gave the feeling of God's presence. Shalu was utterly lost. How many lives does it take to achieve perfection at this level? Shalu could not sleep properly for the next whole week.

The final exams were just one month away when Munnu Dada came unexpectedly to take Shalu back to Parmesh Sadan for three days for a marriage proposal. They were sitting in the visitor's room.

"I have already spoken to the warden. We need to leave soon so that we can reach home before night. Tomorrow, we are leaving for Ghaziabad. They have accepted our proposal and want to meet you." Munnu Dada was extremely excited.

"How come we are going to Ghaziabad? Aren't they supposed to come to Etah?" Shalu expressed her annoyance.

"The Boy's mother had an accident, and she cannot move much." Munnu Dada replied.

"These are all excuses. Why can't you delay all this? Don't you know my exams are not far? I am over with the supremacy of man in society. What assurance do you have that they will not reject the proposal? I strongly oppose these traditions. I am not going with you." Shalu was furious.

"I know this family. Ajay, the boy's elder brother, was my classmate. His sister used to attend Bhaiya Uncle's coaching classes. The boy has studied engineering at BHU and works in the public sector. I have met him. It is worth taking a chance. Please, just this time." Munnu Dada begged.

"This is the last time I will agree to such a meeting." Shalu was still upset.

PART 2

THE BOY

7. JOHARI SYNDROME

My name is Atul Johari. I am part of the great JOHARI family that was initially a Saksena family. But due to conflict with the British in India during my grandfather's time, the family switched over to the subbranch of the Saksena Kayasth dynasty. My grandfather, Ram Chandra Saksena, was a Jailor at that time and used to help the independence fighters under his custody. One day, when he came home for lunch break and was having meals with the family, his Orderly arrived. He explained that my grandfather was required back immediately to witness the execution of a prisoner who was a freedom fighter.

My grandfather could not digest this, from food to fatality. He disobeyed. Later, he left the job and suggested that his sons change their surname so they would not suffer. It was a bit late for my father, Prem Shankar Saksena, and his younger brother, Naresh Shankar Saksena. However, the youngest brother became Karuna Shankar Johari. From then onwards, the next generation adopted Johari as their surname.

As we considered ourselves Ace among the Johari clan, all the boys from my generation had their names starting with the alphabet "A", and the girls had their names ending with "A". So, whichever end you looked at, you would find us as number one or ace. I was the youngest in my family, with three brothers, Arun, Ajay, and Abhay and a sister, Renuka, who came after my eldest brother, Arun.

Apart from being the best, another essential trait of our Johari family that distinguished us from being a typical middle-class family was that most males from our closely knitted clan were known for their fury. We were lions of the jungle. No one told us what was right or wrong. What we did was right. We led, and others followed.

My dad was a father figure for his two brothers, as my grandfather died early, and my parents looked after my grandmother and my two uncles after that. He worked very hard to fund the education of my two uncles. My father was the brightest and most handsome in his generation, but luck was not in his favour. After completing his Master's in agriculture, he qualified for the top job that allowed him to join as a Class-One executive officer, but since he was unable to deposit the bond money, he had to let it go.

Later, he started at a senior non-executive level but due to his honesty, hard work, and innovation he ultimately retired as a senior executive officer. He put himself last and looked after everyone else first. He also maintained a strict religious ritual. He was a devotee of Goddess Gayatri and recited the *Gayatri Mantra* 108 times daily. He also established a small prayer room where he had idols of Lord Ram, Lakshman, and Sita. There was also a Shivling. Prayers were performed twice daily, in the morning and evening. His exceptional willpower and discipline for diet, exercise, and meditation kept him going till the age of ninety-three, despite being diabetic since his early thirties.

My mother, Sushila, was an exceptional lady. She was my father's strength. Her dedication, hard work, and sacrifices made my parents leaders among the extended family. My mother was from a renowned advocate family from the Pratapgarh district in Uttar Pradesh, the Northern part of India. My maternal grandfather was a criminal lawyer and was rated the best among the criminal lawyers of the city. He built a huge house on a large piece of land, where he planted many fruit trees, and created a small poultry farm on the campus.

My mother had four brothers and two sisters, making them seven siblings altogether. Though my mother did not get much formal education like other ladies of that time, but she had a keen sense of good and evil. Her money management skills were exceptional. Among all the financial crises, she saved some money and kept it in various hideouts which was made available when most required. She did all the house work and cooked the best food in the world but would eat last, and only if food was still left. She faced many medical challenges but never visited any doctor. Based on my father's request, my youngest uncle, a doctor, looked after her from afar.

Like my father, my mother also developed religious rituals. She was a devotee of Lord Hanuman and went through *Sunder Kand*, a chapter from Ramayan, as a daily routine. She knew it by heart. She rarely had any spare time but whenever she did, she would read about homoeopathic medicines. She had also developed an interest in Astrology and had a few books that she occasionally referred to. She had a register full of notes and details of the family members' horoscopes. She told me that I had *Kal Sarp Yog* in my horoscope. I did not know much about its meaning, but it titillated me as it was related to a horrible, poisonous snake. Oh, no one would dare take a chance with me unless they wanted to die an untimely death.

My mother had also told me that as per my horoscope, I was a *Manglik*, which again I would twist the word and proudly say, so I am a *Jungli* (uncultured). I always enjoyed projecting myself as an uncultured and dangerous boy, like a poisonous snake, who is best if left alone. Unlike my siblings, I spent most of my time studying. When I needed a short break, I stood close to my mother in the kitchen and watched her cook food for all of us.

I was grateful yet guilty to watch her working so hard. I could not help her. There were no gas stoves. The food was cooked on fireplaces that produced more smoke than heat. Food was cooked while sitting on the ground. The utensils became black with smoke, and it was challenging to clean them. I developed extreme respect and obligation for my mother, who went through this torturous routine twice daily to selflessly feed all of us.

My mother found her existence within my father. She never attempted to establish her separate identity. Whatever my father decided, she abided by it. Though this was a good thing for me, as there has to be a hierarchy for a successful team, but apparently, there was a missing element of participation, or it was not visible to me.

A true leader allows full participation and creates an atmosphere where all the team members are courageous enough to express themselves. A decision should result from the most positive values and be capable of navigating through negative suggestions or risks. The fear factor of the Johari syndrome did not allow this. None of us, including my mother, dared to stand our ground in front of my father to make some significant impact. My mother once told my wife, Shalu, that she had always wore clothes of my father's choice.

My eldest brother, Arun, was fair, gentle, handsome, and intelligent. We used to call him Dada. He was about ten years older than me. That year, he would complete his Bachelor of Science with majors in Zoology and Botany. He had appeared in the combined entrance examination of the entire state of Uttar Pradesh medical colleges. This was his first attempt, and if he succeeded, he would become a doctor in five years. We were sure he would easily qualify with a good rank, but the result did not say so. He missed by three numbers.

This year, the Government changed the policy, and the quota for reserved seats was almost tripled. Candidates from the reserved quota were through even when they scored only ten percent of my brother's marks. My brother could not take this shock. This impacted his mental balance. At that time, Psychiatry was not advanced in India. Arun suffered from this for the rest of his life until one day, he took his life after my father retired. Dada could not contemplate the financial burden that my father would undergo with only half the earnings after retirement. The Sun (Arun) had set untimely for our family.

Next to my eldest brother, Arun, was my elder sister, Renuka. We used to call her *Jijji*. She was very fair and attractive. She was gentle and content. Like my mother, she was short. She was average in her studies but compensated for it with her social skills and polite attitude. The search for her partner started when she was completing her Master's in Arts. I was young at that time, and this process was quite unsettling. Though these boys were no match for my sister, they rejected her or demanded unreasonable dowry. In one instance, my father was so hurt and upset that he decided that by the end of the year, he would ensure that my sister's marriage was settled.

He kept his word. All of us were happy with the match. The boy, Rajiv, was an Engineer and had a good job in Gauhati, the capital of Assam, a Northeast state in India. As we all lived in Uttar Pradesh which was far, I was excited about the possibility of visiting a new state with the additional charm of a two-day-long train journey. I was unhappy with the financial burden that this marriage had put on my parents and the emotional trauma of unnecessary rejections that my sister had to go through.

I decided then that I would have no demands for my marriage, and the ceremony would be straightforward, if possible. Ideally, it would be a court marriage in the presence of the two families. More importantly, I would accept the first serious proposal for my marriage and not reject a girl after the first formal meeting. For me, marriage was a lifelong friendship which should be built on respect and care. There was no scope for an elaborate checklist. It was not a trade. It should be fair and equal. Marriage is a long journey and requires trust between two people and two families.

Next to my sister, Renuka, was my elder brother, Ajay Ji. He was bold and outgoing. He had a mechanical brain and enjoyed putting his hands on any faulty equipment. He was good at dismantling things, even if he could not assemble them back. He had taken the initiative to share most of the household work that was outside the home. This involved buying vegetables, milk, and other necessary items from the market. This probably did not leave much time or interest towards studies, or he had realised that to succeed in life, it was crucial to be worldly wise rather than to be good at studies.

He knew that the education system, at best, would only prepare students for getting a job. He wanted to be his own boss. He tried utilising the experience, exposure, and contacts which he had built through friendships to set up a contracting business for the construction industry.

My dad had told me that when Ajay Ji was just an infant, he used to have high fever with convulsions. Medically, this is not good and should be avoided as it has long-term implications on concentration and focus, thereby impacting many routine activities, that included studies.

Ajay Ji told me another interesting story. It seems that when he was young, a fortune teller had told him that he would not live for long. So, he wanted to make full use of his short life, and thus he felt that there was much more to do than just studies. For the same reason, he did not like much interference in his way of life, especially from his two younger brothers and would quickly lose his temper. Abhay Ji and I feared him and teamed up to save ourselves from his wrath.

Abhay Ji was hardly two years older than me. He was skinny and of the same height and complexion as Ajay Ji. He had a perfect sense of humour, which indicated that he had a very sharp brain. He knew it was not about survival of the fittest but the survival of the wittiest. One who understands the situation and knows well enough what NOT to do instead of an idiot like me, who would get into action without knowing what needs to be done.

This nature made Abhay Ji a happy-go-lucky person. He was creative and always had a strong logic for what he had done or would do. It was after many years that I understood the secret of his unparalleled success when I read that a genius only does what needs to be done and nothing more. At times, Abhay Ji shared his next invention on which he had been working within his mind. Once he succeeded, he could lead a wealthy life from the royalties earned from his research.

It is hard to be unbiased when talking about myself, Atul, the youngest. However, I will try my best. I will focus on what my older siblings have shared about me or the memories of events that remain vivid. I was a *Gora Bhaiya* (fair complexion baby) with relatively prominent eyes and a long neck. My eyes are not black but somewhat a mix of green and brown, or you can call them hazel. From the time of my conception, the process of separating my parents had begun.

My father was shortlisted for a long-term research project in England. Within a week of my birth, he was on his way to England, leaving my mother with the enormous task of looking after the whole family and her mother-in-law. In those days, there were no means of communication thus no support whatsoever. My mother was brave, and I would hide in her arms for comfort and courage.

Among my earliest memories, apart from being picked up for the school bus by the attendant lady, who would come running up to our street and scream, "Come on Chunnu Bhaiya, come on Munnu Bhaiya". This was a call for my elder brother Abhay Ji and me as we attended the same school. Raghuvir Bal Mandir was an English medium school in Aligarh, where we were admitted due to pressure from my father's colleagues to have a bright future and better opportunities. The public schools were hopeless, but there was no other choice if you could not afford the fees.

At times, when we were a little early for school, we would walk some fifty metres from our narrow street to the main road to get to our school bus stop. There was also a local shopping strip with vegetable shops and grocery stores. Here, I had often witnessed a young boy, about eighteen years old, with no clothes and roaming around, completely lost. I wondered: "Who was he? Where was his family? Why was he like this?" At times, he would have a carrot in his hand, which the keeper of the vegetable shop might have given to him. However, it did not make much sense to him.

Occasionally, I also saw him wearing a shirt that he had already torn, and the next day, again, it would not be there. Whenever I saw that young boy, I felt a sense of great confusion and fear. To this day, I have such a vivid recollection of his innocent face. May God never punish anyone so harshly. May God give us the courage and light to build a society where no one is so alone that they are unaware of their soul. I have grown up, and we live in a much more developed society. Now, people need many more clothes, multiple layers of clothing, to hide their bodies or their sins.

8. GURU JI

From this time onward, I retained most of my memories. I had completed class two, and it was the early months of class three when my father was transferred from Aligarh to Lucknow. Fortunately, we did not have to look for a house thanks to my elder uncle, Naresh. It was a small colony with only eight blocks, and each block had four apartments, two on the ground level and two on the first floor. Only government executives could be allocated these apartments by pulling some influential strings.

Just across the road was a school named Saraswati Sishu Mandir. As the name suggested, it was for young kids, from class one to five. Both boys and girls studied there. My father was sitting in the Principal's office, Mr Tej Pal Sethi Ji, who had an impressive personality. Tall, fair, thin structured, wearing a white *dhoti-kurta*, a typical Hindu outfit.

"I have two sons who I would like to be part of your institution. I am sure you will not be disappointed. We have been transferred from Aligarh and live just across the street. I am in a transferable government service, and it would be very kind if you could accommodate them in the middle of the session." My father spoke in a persuasive but confident tone and handed over our progress reports from the previous school.

Mr Tej glanced over the progress reports and nodded, "Class three for Atul and Class four for Abhay, but we need a quick assessment of them."

"That is fine with me. You can review them, but I want Atul to be in class two, not three." My father corrected the technicality of the grades.

"I did not quite get it. Have I listened to you correctly?" Mr Tej Pal Sethi looked confused but continued. "Atul has an excellent score, and his reports say he held first rank in grade two; why do you want him to repeat the class?"

"I know Atul was ranked one in his class, and I want him that way in future as well. There is a big shift from his previous school to this school. Your school focuses on Hindi and Sanskrit, but Atul did class two as an English medium student. I want his entire focus in these two subjects so he can still maintain his first rank in the final examination," replied my father.

The argument was great, and the purpose was crystal clear. Mr Tej looked into my eyes with mixed sentiments as if he wanted assurance from me. Can I take this challenge, not just this year, but for the rest of my life? Do I understand that sometimes one must step back to win the battle? Will I spring back to take a big leap forward or get stuck to the back bench? Parents and teachers can only guide us and set the building blocks. It is for us to unravel the mysteries and live our dreams. Time will tell if I met my parents' expectations or lost energy halfway through the race.

On my first day at the new school, I reported to the Principal's office. I had to wait there as Mr Tej was on rounds to ensure that all the classes were going well and there were no issues. When he came back, he confirmed my classroom and provided directions. It was the second room from the left corner. The class had already started when I reached the door and so I stopped there.

"May I come in, Sir?" I addressed in a firm and somewhat loud voice.

All eyes turned towards me. The class teacher paused in mid-sentence and turned his attention to me. There was pin-drop silence and an atmosphere of total confusion, as if an alien was standing at the door. Suddenly, a child jumped out of the back bench and approached me, almost running and spoke in Hindi:

"*Ye Sir nahi hain, inhe Aacharya Ji kaho*".

"I don't call my elders and teachers by their names," I responded irritably. Nobody tells me what is right or wrong. Johari blood ran in my veins.

"No, you got me wrong. It is not his name. It is how everyone calls the teachers." The boy clarified with a bit of a winning smile on his face. I was not convinced, but I knew something was wrong. It could not be settled right now, so, I corrected my sentence:

"May I come in, please?" This time, I skilfully avoided the address.

"Please, come in," the teacher replied. However, the young

child was still standing in my way and had no intention of getting out of the way.

"My name is Raghvendra. Will you be my friend?" the boy asked, giving his introduction.

"No". I replied straight and firmly. Our eyes were locked again. I continued with the explanation for rejecting his proposal. "I know that if someone approaches too quickly, then he is not a good person. We cannot be friends." The boy returned to his desk, disappointed. The teacher pointed to an empty desk in the middle row. I took my place, and the class resumed. Already, I had broken one heart and the norms of the classroom or probably the norms of the school. The message was clear: I would be the one who would pick, choose, and decide what was right. You better agree with me, or you would have to be on your own.

The class tests were due in a month and were approaching fast. Nobody reached me for friendship; after all, who would like to be friends with such a rude boy? Though I needed friends, I was not scared of being left out. I had always been a somewhat lonely planet. Finally, the tests for all subjects were over, and each teacher read out the scores in their class. I had done well. I got a full score in all subjects except Hindi and Sanskrit, where I had not even opened my account. Zero and zero. I had started calling the teachers Acharya Ji, but always with some hesitation and a little effort, as if I was disrespecting them.

The next set of tests was another three months away. I showed slight improvement. I scored two out of ten in Hindi but had yet to open my account in Sanskrit. I needed to make this up in the final examination, which was just a couple of months away, or I would be repeating class two again. Finally, the ordeal came, and I made it—a hundred out of a hundred in Hindi and Sanskrit.

I had ultimately got my head around the subjects as well as the school's culture. All the boys and girls in school were brothers and sisters. In the morning, we chanted long rhymes in Sanskrit before the school prayer and not-so-long rhymes before lunch break. I had opened up a bit and showed respect to my other classmates; after all, they were my brothers and sisters. However, I maintained a distance from Raghavendra and the other backbench students.

I was now in class three and was gaining ground. I also participated in cultural and sports activities and did well. Among sports, we had Kho-Kho, Kabaddi, Racing, Shooting, and Jumping through the fire ring. My brother, Abhay Ji, was good at Shooting and Jumping through the Fire Ring. He was the sports secretary. I avoided the fire ring, and could not comprehend the trick of aiming in Shooting. I could run fast but could not beat the much shorter boy. This was a paradox to me. I had to be satisfied with second place.

Being fearless helped me in leading the Kabaddi team and make it win every time, even in the interstate meet of Saraswati Sishu Mandir schools. I did well in the School Band. It was like a military band. Among the cultural and literary activities, I excelled in storytelling, handwriting, and essay writing. By default, I was in every activity as captain or vice-captain. Most boys and girls became friendly with me, but some still had reservations, especially those from wealthy families. Probably, they felt that I had stolen their deserving spot or their fundamental right to be number one. If God was in their favour, why did I not respect them?

By the time I completed class four, my popularity was at its peak. My classmates nicknamed me Guru Ji. Mr Tej was transferred and was replaced by Mr Harishankar Kashyap as Principal. He was tall but a little bulky. He was calm and considerate. Once, he took our class to the garden within the school campus, where there were quite a few guava trees and some mango trees. This area was somewhat separated from the main playground, and students were not allowed there, though it was the favourite place for some students who lived nearby and stole the fruits after school hours. Harishankar Ji took us from tree to tree, pointing out the different fruits and telling us the secret of identifying the ripe and sweet guavas from the rest that looked equally green:

"Can you see this fruit? Though it is green, it has smooth and shiny skin. You can feel this one and the one next to it. You can feel that the other one is rough. Both seem equally hard. Try to pick both, and you will find that the shiny one comes out relatively easily." He looked at one of the younger students as if he was encouraging him to try.

The boy followed his instructions. He inspected the two fruits keenly with his eyes and hands and then plucked both. It was a bit of an effort to pick the second one, which looked rough. We all took turns inspecting the two fruits and passing them on to the next student. The final test was to taste them which was done by the student who first picked them from the tree. His expressions were enough and needed no further explanation. Harishankar Ji smiled. He knew we all had resolved the mystery and were waiting for his next move. He continued:

"You can each pick one fruit, but make sure you pick the right one. Call me if you are unsure before picking, and I will help you." He then moved away a little to watch the thrill and excitement that we all were going through. He had achieved his objective with his unconventional approach. He had established that he was approachable, but at the same time, he had earned our respect. He knew that from now on those among us who were stealing the fruits after hours would only pick the right fruits, and the damage would be minimal.

Our new class teacher was Mr Ajay Ji, who had recently been transferred to our school. Mr Ajay Ji verified the enrolment of all the class four students in the first class of the session. He asked the students to stand up when their names were called. This was to help familiarise himself with each student. As my name was called, I stood up. Ajay Ji looked at me and nodded his head in confirmation with a low voice:

"Atul Johari".

"No Aacharya Ji, his name is Guru Ji. He is Guru Ji", it was a combined voice from a few students.

"Guru Ji, Guru Ji, Guru Ji..." The boys kept chanting simultaneously, beating the desk rhythmically with their palms.

"Ok, I am fixing the name". Replied Mr Ajay Ji, writing Guru Ji next to my name in the register. All the boys had a winning smile on their faces. I was embarrassed and confused with my new official identity. I wondered what was more important, my name or my title. Why were my classmates so excited about branding me as Guru Ji? Had they found another layer between them and the teachers? Why was this extra layer so important to them? Did everyone want someone to fill the gap between them and the next person in charge? Did it make their life somewhat simpler or more enjoyable? Is this why many spiritual leaders, Babas or Gurus, exist in society today?

Although our class teacher, Ajay Ji, did not teach any specific subject, but he had a far more significant role to fulfil. To develop our personalities. To make us good citizens. To fill us with morals, excitement, and curiosity. He told us stories about our great leaders, Gandhi Ji, Nehru Ji, Subhash Chandra Bose, Chandra Shekhar Azad, Bhagat Singh, and many more. Stories from mythology about Lord Ram, Lord Krishna.

These immortal stories, the rabbit and the lion, the fox and the heron, the deaf frog and many more. All these stories shaped me from inside. These stories were real for me. Will I be able to stick with truth like Gandhi Ji? Could I become bold like Bhagat Singh, organised like Subhash Chandra Bose, clever like the rabbit, and focused like the deaf frog?

It was the start of fifth grade, my final year in this school. Abhay Ji joined the Government Jubilee Inter College with my older brother, Ajay Ji. A state meet of all Sishu Mandir schools was scheduled this year. The state meet was held every fifth year. Luckily, this time, the venue was Lucknow, though it was not in our school campus. The meet would last five days. All of us were requested to confirm our names and agree to pay a fee of Rupees fifty. This was a considerable amount then, and I knew that my parents could not afford it.

It was evident that only a few students from wealthy backgrounds could pay this sum. I had clarified to all the students in my class that I would not be attending the meet. I could not put my parents in this financial crisis. Most students agreed to follow me and skip the meet. Few wealthier students dared not go against the masses, so they also decided in our favour. Only three days were left to confirm the nominations, and no student from our class had confirmed despite repeated reminders. Finally, our Principal, took the initiative and invited our class to see him. The next day, our class sat on the lawn beside our classroom, facing Principal Harishankar Ji, who was sitting in a chair. It was a sunny, pleasant day.

"I have not received nominations for the state meet from your class. I am here to answer questions and get started. Please ask now so we can finalise. Raise your hands if you plan to go to the meet." This was a firm call from the head of the school.

My face was down, and my eyes were fixed on the ground. There was utter silence. I lifted my head slightly and rolled my eyes to gauge the response, but I could barely see the boys sitting beside me. They were also looking down with their hands clasped tightly.

"Someone needs to tell me why none of you have responded to my call. After all, if you do not tell me, how can I help you?" Explained Harishankar Ji.

"Guru Ji is not going to the meet." A boy replied hesitantly.

"I am asking all of you to tell me about yourselves, rather than about someone else." Responded Harishankar Ji in an irritated tone.

"We cannot go without Guru Ji." Replied another boy with his eyes fixed on the Principal.

"So, who is this Guru Ji you are referring to?" Harishankar Ji clearly showed his ignorance, undermining anyone else's authority against the head of the institution.

All eyes turned towards me. I was still facing down, firm, emotionless, and fearless. There was silence around me.

"He is our Guru Ji." The boy beside me finally broke the spell and tapped on my shoulder.

"Will you tell me something, GURU Ji? What is the matter? Why does no one want to go?" Asked Harishankar Ji, facing me.

"The fee is too high. My parents cannot afford it. Thus, I am unable to attend the meet. I am not preventing anyone else from going." I made my stand clear. I emphasised that I had not pressurised the other students and that they could choose whether to go or stay.

"Ok, I am prepared to reduce the fees to Rupees forty. What do you think, boys and girls?"

No one responded.

"I cannot go below Rupees thirty-five. Those who want to go, please raise your hand." Said Harishankar Ji.

Two hands went up. Both were girls from wealthy families, keen to show their independence and strength. All the other students were anxious but backed me up firmly.

"Tell me, Guru Ji, what do you think is the right fee for this five-day state meet." Harishankar Ji addressed me after a long pause, when he did not receive any more nominations.

"Rupees fifteen." I had stretched my limit from Rupees ten to fifteen. I was not enjoying the conversation and wanted to finish it quickly.

Harishankar Ji looked towards the sky to hide his anger and frustration. He closed his eyes and went into deep thought. From Rupees fifty to fifteen was a long way.

"Let us settle down at Rupees twenty. You all should be happy now." Harishankar Ji was almost ready to get up from his chair, convinced that this would be the last call. Unfortunately, no one moved, they looked at me for approval. I was undisturbed.

"I have already stretched my limit," I responded, then turned my face towards the students. "If any of you is comfortable with the proposal, please let him know. I do not want to stand between you and the meet."

The students looked at me with sad faces and turned their faces towards the ground without responding. Once again, it was a stalemate.

Harishankar Ji stood up from his chair and looked around to read the faces of all the students. He could sense that no one was prepared to leave their Guru Ji behind. The lion was helpless before the herd of tiny elephants that had decided not to leave any of its members behind. The two girls who had raised their hands earlier felt outcast and exposed and tried to deny their earlier acceptance of the offer.

"Well, I accept the offer. Rupees fifteen. Can we have a count now?"

All hands went up. The boys sitting next to me lifted my hands along with theirs. Everyone was cheering. I was overwhelmed by the support and solidarity shown by my classmates. We would bring every award to our school. No one could beat us. We were the Team. We were One. A Strong One.

It had been about two months since the state meet was over. Our class had made a clean sweep in all the events. However, it left a terrible taste in the mouths of the school's governing body. The Principal, Harishankar Ji, and our class teacher, Ajay Ji, were transferred and replaced by Jitender Ji as Principal and Mahesh Ji as our class teacher. The agenda was clear: to reestablish the teachers' supremacy and recover the financial losses. I was the thorn in Mahesh Ji's eye. He wanted to set me right, and he finally got an opportunity.

My grandmother, who lived with us, died late one night. Though I did not have much connection with her, a death within the family was a first experience for me. I was lost. The body was kept on three big ice bricks to preserve it till all close relatives could arrive for the last seeing. Each time a new relative came, the surroundings were filled with screams and loud cries. Cremation was over by the next day. I remained sad and confused for a few days. Often, I cried myself to sleep at night, but I did not make it obvious to anyone. This impacted my routine, and I could not even complete my homework.

"Bring your homework notebook and the textbook." Commanded Mahesh Ji, standing in front of the classroom. He had observed over the last few days, that I was somewhat lost and must have guessed that I was unprepared for this. I looked in my bag; the textbook was missing. I knew my homework was incomplete.

"Come here quick with whatever you have got." Shouted Mahesh Ji with anger. When I reached him, he snatched my notebook, opened it, and screamed:

"No homework for the last two days and no textbook. You lazy, dumb boy. What do you think of yourself? I must teach you a lesson so no one takes such a liberty." He started beating and slapping me. He went mad. He was swearing and throwing his hands everywhere, hitting me. This was not the norm of the school.

This had never happened. All the students were shocked. Mahesh Ji proved a point. After he stopped, he looked at everyone in the classroom as if he was challenging them. *"Is there anyone who wants to help this boy?"* There was no Guru Ji now. There was just another young boy, helpless, broken, and dusted.

Later, after class, some students reached out to Principal Jitender Ji, but he was not interested. He asked everyone to attend the class and not interfere. Prakash Narayan, a student in my class, was unhappy with the events. His father was a Police Inspector. The next day, I noticed some unusual activity in school. His father, accompanied Prakash Narayan in his Police Uniform. He placed his hand over his pistol and shouted, "Take me to that teacher, and I will take care of him." Soon after, the teachers and the Principal surrounded him and tried to calm him down. Mahesh Ji was nowhere to be seen. The Principal assured him that this would never happen again and that he would take disciplinary action.

Mahesh Ji was not our class teacher anymore. We never faced each other again. No boy was ever beaten again, yet the battle was not over. It was the time of Cold War. Teachers started promoting Krishna Kumar Jaiswal, who had consistently held second rank in class after me. The Jaiswal family had donated a couple of Godrej Almirahs to the school, apart from other financial favours which we were unaware of. This year, all the fifth-year boys would be ranked in the entire state, and Krishna Kumar must stand first in the state, not just in our class. The teachers were confident that the next five months would be enough to achieve this target, especially when Krishna Kumar was not part of any extracurricular activities.

Before I finished my classes at this school and departed forever, I want to share one last story. I sensed that I was not liked anymore. Instead, I was the black sheep. It must have impacted me in some way. I had always enjoyed being a lonely planet, but being outcast or an obstacle was weakening my soul. Despite what was going on, I had done well in my half-yearly exams, and my father had bought me a beautiful fountain pen of my choice. Writing with a fountain pen was a privilege for class five students.

It was a grey pen with a bright red tip on the cap and the same bright red tailpiece on the body. This was my first fountain pen, and I was over the moon with it. However, on the second day at school, I lost it. I looked around everywhere, asked a couple of boys in my class, and then started crying. It was unusual and shocking for the teachers, and one of them was sympathetic towards me. He asked me to describe the pen and then instructed the other students to show them their pens. After a few turns, a young-looking student came up with a pen that was like the one I had. However, it was not new and had been chewed from the top and bottom.

"It was like this." I stopped sobbing and said.

"Is this the pen, or was your's like this?" The teacher wanted confirmation.

"This is my pen." I hesitated and then replied.

The teacher took the pen from the student and gave it to me. The boy cried and insisted that this was his pen, but I took the pen without making eye contact with the boy. I had cheated. I had shamed myself. I had sold my soul. I had disappointed myself. I had betrayed myself. I lost this pen again within a day or two, but I was not sad now. I had lost everything I had anyway. I was filled with guilt. I wanted to apologise to the boy, but I did not have the courage. I promised myself that I would never repeat this in future. I would not take anyone's share. I would only give, not take. The pain of taking was unbearable for me. I beg:

"If you are the boy reading my story, please pardon me. I'm sorry. I did not have the courage to tell the truth. The Guru Ji had died. The one you all supported had betrayed you. I do not wish to show you my face again."

When the Class Five results were announced, I secured second position, ranking behind Krishna Kumar by a considerable margin. He also ranked first in the whole state. I was ranked thirteenth in the state. Looking back, I realised that life had taught me a perfect lesson without making me pay dearly.

Every institution is made for a bigger purpose. If you stand in between, you may even lose your life. If you do not like the ideals of an institution, you make yourself a better person by raising yourself above the institution but you do not try to change the institution.

It is a significant community. It serves a bigger community. It is there to create a balance between two opposite ends. If there is an imbalance of unacceptable levels, the institution dies, and a new and better one will arise. Nature has its own rules. It prevails. You need to just mind your nature.

9. DISTRICT ETAH

After finishing fifth grade, the challenge was to find a new school in a nearby locality with a good reputation and without being expensive. In short, we were looking for value for money. Through one of my father's colleagues, Tandon uncle, we found out about Mahanagar Boys School which offered education in both Hindi and English. It was not easy to get admission due to its high standard of English. This was a Convent school where teachers were addressed as brothers and sisters. In the last four years, my English language had taken a toll. It would be a miracle if I got through the entrance examination, but it was worth trying.

My performance in English was not good, and that was enough entertainment for Malti aunty. This would certainly keep her happy until my entrance examination results were declared. The results were out, and I disappointed Malti aunty. I was in, and so was Krishna Kumar, my fellow mate from Saraswati Sishu Mandir. We were the only two from our previous school. Either I had done well in other subjects, or the examiner was overwhelmed by my sense of humour. In the selection list, there was another name that caught my attention: Kirti. How come Kirti was selected in this boys' school?

Kirti Narendra was my classmate in Saraswati Sishu Mandir. She was among the two girls who belonged to a wealthy family and had stood against me during the episode with Principal Harishankar Ji. She was fair and had curly hair, which were always neatly cut to shoulder length. She did not like me and had always tried to show me down, even when I was negotiating the fee for the state meet with Harishankar Ji, the Principal. On the first day in Class six, I found that Kirti was a short, fair, and thin boy. Will this boy carry the same rivalry against me? I was a bit sceptical. I was also happy to have the opportunity to level the ground with Krishna Kumar, who had left me behind in the final exams of Class Five.

I worked hard to make my place among the boys of this new class. If only two boys from my previous school could make it to this school, all the other boys would be equally capable and give me a tough time. I was disappointed with my English performance in the entrance exam and wanted to improve. The results of the quarterly exams were out. Chandra Prakash Goyal, a thin, somewhat dark and slim boy, had claimed the first position with a significant margin of about four percent to the second place held by Krishna Kumar Jaiswal. In the third place was Bhupender Singh Nayal; again, the gap was about another four percent.

Bhupender was a handsome, fair, well-built, muscular boy. By nature, he was quiet. He had been studying in an Army school. Such schools were known for extracurricular activities like horse riding, swimming, and other field sports, apart from having high education standards. Why someone had to change from such an excellent institution was unknown. I was at the fourth rank, only by a slight margin. This was the only consolation for me. The first and second places looked out of reach. I had my focus set on the third place. Bhupender would not give his place easily; he had the blood of an army officer. Even more frustrating was that Krishna Kumar was one year younger than me, and Chandra Prakash was two years younger than me.

Bhupender had a few friends who shadowed him around. Kirti was one of them. Due to my extreme competition with Bhupender, his friends, which included Kirti, started disliking me. This gang always took the opposite side to me in a team game or a sport and often targeted me by sledging. In this process, they often won.

I was no longer a sports person or keen to participate in extracurricular activities. My focus was to study and get the third rank. Anil Tandon, Tandon uncle's son, was a champion in General Knowledge. He had won competitions at school and district level. Apart from General Knowledge, which was not part of any curriculum, his favourite subjects were History and Geography. I considered General Knowledge a distraction and never bothered to pick up the newspaper or listen to the news. History and Geography were my soft spots. Any subject which required the use of memory was an uphill task for me. I was not clumsy in sketching and painting, but it was not my cup of tea. Though I was self-motivated for studies, my father still set an award for taking the whole family out for a movie if I got the first rank in class.

I was aware that with so many subjects being my weak areas, I would never be able to get to the first spot. I was in Class Eight and wanted to crack the first place. I persuaded Anil Tandon to provide his notes on History from Class Eight, which he had passed with the highest marks the previous year. I also mastered sketching and painting, which were likely to come in the exam. All this help and preparation did the trick, and in the quarterly exams, I surprised everyone by scoring the first rank. Though this did not last long, it was enough to give me a ray of hope.

At home, my father was proud. He asked me to choose a film to watch over the weekend. Everyone in the house shared their recommendations for their preferred movie. There was a section in the newspaper where all the film screenings were listed. I wanted to know my mother's choice so I could do her a favour. She happily pointed out one of the religious movies, *"Hari Darshan"*. This was the movie about Prince Prahlad, a devotee of Lord Vishnu. His father was a staunch enemy of Lord Vishnu.

Being a religious movie, the government had exempted it from entertainment tax, thus the tickets were almost half price. It was the right choice for me. I could please my mother while alleviating the financial burden on my father. However, this was a significant disappointment for the rest of the family—my brothers and sister—who were eager to watch an action film. I enjoyed the film, and so did my mother. I felt proud and content that I could do something for my mother and make her a little happier.

I worked full throttle to maintain my first rank for the rest of the year, but I already had some setbacks. CP Goyal claimed first place. Krishna Kumar and Bhupender had yet to catch up. The Final exams were only a few weeks away, and the competition was at its peak. The Final exams had fifty percent weightage. The rest was based on the scores achieved throughout the year. The Final exams were starting the next day, and I was running a high fever, which made me feel helpless and defeated.

Based on the medical certificate, I knew I would be promoted to the next class. However, I hated the word promoted or grace.

Except for one subject, I had scored above thirty-three out of fifty in my yearly performance, and if I could somehow appear in this subject and score above five marks out of fifty, I would have a clear pass. No grace marks. No Promotion. Clear pass.

My parents did not want me to sit for the exams, but they agreed for this subject. I could hardly attempt two questions and left the paper unfinished. I was satisfied with passing the grade with clear marks. I had already witnessed the joy experienced by Kirti and gang, who had put up a dance show while hurling their books in the air when I had come to sit in the only exam to save myself from the shame of promotion or pass with grace marks.

Soon after my Class Eight results, the UP Board High School results were out in the newspaper. My elder brother Abhay Ji passed with first division. This was somewhat unexpected. For the last few generations, no one in our family had passed high school with first division. It was expected that either I would break this record or Anoop, the youngest son of Naresh uncle would have this privilege. Our family was filled with joy. Abhay Ji had proven himself. From this point onwards, no one would underestimate Abhay Ji, and his name would be taken with respect.

The last few years had been tough for my parents. Quite a few relatives came to stay with us due to health issues and educational prospects, which put extra financial burden on us. Though Naresh uncle and his family were in Lucknow and were much better off, they preferred to keep themselves at arm's length.

Malti aunty and Naresh uncle visited us, but the meetings were often unpleasant. This could be due to very different perspectives or financial status. Probably, they were also sceptical that we might not handover the house we were staying in, which was allocated under their name. At times, Malti aunty would provoke my mother, but as my father never wanted her to react, she restrained her emotions. Sometimes, when my mother could not control her feelings, she fainted, especially after my uncle and aunt had gone.

My father was finding it hard to keep his blood sugar under control despite exercises and extensive diet control. He had a wound in his right leg, which was not healing and which was quite deep. It was excruciating to clean and dress it. Though Naresh uncle had a personal car, which he used to commute to office that was adjacent to my father's office, my father never asked for a lift and continued to commute on his push bike. I found it a bit odd and imagined myself in the same situation. Would I do the same if God ever put me in a privileged position? Amid all this confusing environment, one thing was clear: we were being trained by life within a controlled family environment instead of being thrown naked into unfamiliar territory.

By the time my father recovered from his injury and got control of his blood sugar, my mother had become the victim of a chronic disease. She was diagnosed with Tuberculosis of the uterus. Medically, she had to undergo treatment for at least one year, which constituted a cocktail of antibiotics. Instead, she was operated on to remove her uterus. My mother suffered its complications for the rest of her life.

During these years, our family had two more setbacks. My eldest brother Arun marginally missed out on the Medical Entrance Examination, MBBS. He gradually started drifting towards depression. It became apparent only when his bathing time started exceeding an hour. He remained increasingly anxious. He would keep walking around the house instead of resting or settling at his study table. He avoided going out and preferred to stay aloof. My Doctor Uncle, Karuna Ji, diagnosed it as the onset of some mental disorder and suggested medical advice. This pushed our family into a deep crisis.

At the same time, Phupha Ji, who was the husband of my father's sister, Pushpa Ji, was brought in a poor condition in an ambulance, to our home He had blood stains all over his white clothes. He had jumped out from a running train. He had been suffering from depression for some time, which had gone unnoticed. Fortunately, he only suffered minor injuries, which left no trace within a few weeks. However, it took another few months for him to recover completely from the depression.

Arun Dada told us that he had been praying to God to cure Phupha Ji, even at the cost of his own health, as he had a large family to care for. All this was cooking inside me. Did God accept the prayer of my eldest brother? Did my mother get the correct medical treatment and care? Were we getting fair support from our extended family? Why were we carrying along additional members of our extended family under such hardships? My father had shown unprecedented courage, patience, and endeavour against all odds and won the spot of an ideal man in my heart. Would I ever be able to fit into my father's shoes? Would I be able to put others before my priorities?

Seemingly, there was no end to our hardships and bad luck when my father returned from office one day during the summer vacation with a letter in his hand. He told my mother that he had been transferred to Etah as District Agriculture Officer. He would be the head of the Agriculture Department for the entire district. This was a prestigious posting, and he had to join within a month. Everything had to be packed, uprooted and shifted to a new, unknown place. Call these perks or downsides of a government job, but these are the harsh realities of life.

Naresh uncle told us that we would soon become aware of the actual status of my father's job. Everyone becomes a desk clerk in the head office, but in the district, you get an office, a government vehicle, and servants to help with household chores. He also cautioned us that Etah district was renowned for dacoits and was not a safe place. We would have to be careful.

Naresh uncle's family was looking forward to moving back into the house where we were staying. I was excited by the thought of a new lease on life and the belief that we would leave behind the evil spell that seemed to surround our family. I was a little sad about leaving the Tandon family. I used to enjoy the company of everyone in their family and had tasted the soft *Parathas* and tasty vegetables a couple of times when Anil and I had swapped our tiffins at school.

The day of shifting came. We were to travel in the same truck along with all the luggage. My father had been meticulously monitoring the loading of all the boxes, furniture, and everything else on the back of the truck to ensure that there would be room for us to sit. Everything was stacked and tied with a rope to avoid movement that could cause breakage and crush any of us sitting behind the luggage. My elder brother Abhay Ji and I sat in the top section of the truck, just above the driver and the front passenger seats. This was like a boxed area without a lid, and the sides only about one and a half feet high. I was thrilled with the idea that I would have a complete panoramic 360-degree view and fresh air.

As the truck was on its way, the driver applied brakes while I was sitting on my knees, enjoying, and chatting with Abhay Ji. The sudden deceleration almost threw me out and in front of the truck. It was a narrow escape, and I was frozen with fear. This was not a safe place, contrary to what I had watched in movies where such places in trucks and buses or even on top of the trains were packed with people singing songs during their journey. On the next opportunity, we left our prestigious spot from the top of the truck and hid behind the back with our elder brother Ajay Ji. I was scared to share this experience with anyone else. A good lesson had been learned: all that is rosy is not good.

As no government house was available in Etah, we were temporarily accommodated at the Aruna Nager Guest House. The luggage was shifted to a nearby warehouse which belonged to the agriculture department. The best part was that my mother did not have to prepare all meals. There was a shared kitchen where the office staff had appointed two cooks.

There was another interesting development: the day we entered Etah, the Prime Minister, Mrs Indira Gandhi, declared a nationwide Emergency. This gave tremendous power to the government machinery. Any antisocial activity could result in punishment and a jail sentence. In other words, we were safe from dacoits to some extent.

Soon, we were allocated a government house. Although it was a level below my father's entitlement, it was much better than staying in the Guest House. This was in the Officer's Colony adjacent to the District Magistrate's campus. There was a big green patch near the colony where peacocks roamed around. We enjoyed the company of other officers' kids who were our age and lived in the nearby houses. I, Abhay Ji, Ajay Ji, and I were admitted to the ASA Inter

College, which had a better rating than the Government College in Etah district.

This was the school where my brother, Ajay Ji, formed a friendship with Sharad Ji, the elder brother of Shalu, who would later become my better half. Their friendship played a key role in settling my marriage and allowed me to enter the prestigious Parmesh Sadan through the front door. I had taken my elder sister, Renuka, to the Parmesh Sadan campus for the coaching classes run by Shalu's youngest uncle. Bhaiya uncle's coaching classes were famous in Etah, where he offered several subjects for Bachelor of Arts (BA) and Master of Arts (MA).

There was no university in Etah. The only degree college was on the outskirts of the main city. No girl preferred it and thus took up higher studies in private. Bhaiya uncle was a teacher at the Government Inter College. However, he had established himself as the best higher education coach in Etah District. His coaching classes were always packed with girls.

The coaching classes were held in a somewhat secluded building which comprised three small rooms in the front right section of Parmesh Sadan. With so many young and attractive girls visiting Parmesh Sadan almost daily, it was hard for Shalu's elder brothers, Sharad Ji (Munnu Dada) and Pradeep Ji (Raju Dada), to contain themselves within the main building and abstain from the pleasure of regularly consuming some eye-tonic.

Tingals, Shalu's cousin brothers, who were the same age as her real brothers, also made best use of these opportunities when visiting Parmesh Sadan during the holidays. At that time, Shalu must have been in Class Three or Four, as she is about four years younger than me. Had we ever noticed each other during this time? This is something I will leave to the imagination of my readers.

Etah was such a small city that it would not be wrong if I said that everyone knew everyone. Bholu Bhaiya was a well-known photographer who specialised in taking photographs of young girls which would go along with their resume for a marriage proposal. As Bholu Bhaiya came on his push bike to provide home service, he was by far, the first choice for this purpose.

My sister, Renuka, was in BA Final, and her age was appropriate for the matrimonial process, so the services of Bholu Bhaiya were called for. A short, chubby, fair person in his early thirties parked his push bike outside our residence and entered our home with his box-like camera. His face was innocent, featureless and expressionless. Maybe this was why he was nicknamed Bholu Bhaiya, Innocent Brother. He took a few shots and promised to deliver the final product within a couple of weeks.

While inspecting the photographs, we found it hard to find a resemblance with our sister. Her face looked featureless in the pictures. One of the photographs was painfully and skilfully coloured manually, as getting a colour photograph at that time was scarce. Now, we understood the secret of his specialization and popularity.

Another outstanding feature of Etah were the sweets. The shop, close to the courts, was famous for its jumbo-sized *Gulab Jamuns*. They were priced at Rupee one each. Despite their large size, they were soft inside, and yet, you dared not challenge yourself with another one unless your roots were from the Priests of Mathura, the birthplace of Lord Krishna. Whenever we lost our cricket match to another team outside the Officer's Club, our captain treated us to these jumbo Gulab Jamuns. His argument was to convert a defeat into a pleasant experience.

Another unique sweet worth mentioning is *Ghevar*. It is a seasonal sweet which is available in the Spring season. It has ruled the hearts of every citizen of Etah. It comes in a disk shape, where the base is made of a crispy and porous mixture of flour and ghee that is soaked in sugar syrup and a top layer of cream in exotic flavours.

Apart from this, you could find fresh *Samosa* shops at every cross-section throughout the city. The soil of Etah was especially suited for producing peanuts, and large piles of top-quality peanuts could be seen in the markets. This is where I developed my taste for peanuts, especially when fried and tossed with different spices. Owing to their availability and low price, Peanuts are the preferred dry fruit for those with limited means, even though they possess nearly the same protein content as the other dry fruits.

By any standard, the ASA Inter College looked no better than a ruin. Apart from a few classrooms that looked like rooms, most had tin roofs. The campus was big, but the fields were bare, without any traces of grass. Most of the boys were from the nearby villages and seemed to have no concerns for education. The teachers looked tired and uninterested. The education level was appalling. Once again, I was undisputed, unchallenged, and the best. It looked like the teachers were no match and were somewhat scared of me. This led me only one way: downhill.

The Officer's Colony was the only place that was somewhat developed and cultured. Close to the Officer's Colony was an Officer's Club with some gaming facilities like Table Tennis and Carrum Board. Officers and their kids would come here in the evening to socialise. Our tenure for Etah was limited to roughly eighteen months, which coincided with the state of Emergency.

After this, my father was transferred to Gorakhpur, an Eastern district of the state. Etah contributed positively to my personality. I developed tremendous confidence, probably overconfidence. I started looking smart, laughed like a child with no inhibitions, and expressed myself without fear. We were well-treated wherever we went with our father, which made us proud. We found our breed. We were not sheep. We were lions.

Political activities were picking up pace just before the Emergency was lifted. The federal election was overdue. The Chief Minister of Uttar Pradesh, Mr Hemwati Nandan Bahuguna, was to visit Etah. Apart from getting a glance at the Chief Minister, I was keen to see his helicopter landing from close. This piece of machinery was a big puzzle to me. How could such a heavy machine fly straight up from the ground? I was told that a helicopter could fly in any direction, even backwards, stay still in the air, and hover.

I watched the insect Dragon Fly with amazement, like it was nature's helicopter. With extreme excitement, I observed the helicopter landing and looked at the Chief Minister with a bit of jealousy. In person, he looked the same as he did in his photos. I was unaware that Mr Bahuguna would stay in Parmesh Sadan during his brief trip to Etah.

Following Mr Bahuguna's visit, the Prime Minister, Mrs Indira Gandhi, was scheduled to visit Etah and would be received by Shalu's mother as chief of the welcome team. Both Mr Bahuguna and Mrs Indira Gandhi were from the Congress Party, and Shalu's parents were strong allies of the opposition political party, Jan Sangh. Still, Shalu's elder Uncle Illa, who supported Congress, was pleased to have Shalu's mother, Saroj, as the head of the welcome team. In a couple of weeks, Atal Ji, the president of Jan Sangh, visited Etah and spent time with Shalu's parents at Parmesh Sadan, to discuss strategies for the upcoming elections. This was the prestige, and status that Parmesh Sadan held in Etah district.

10. REALITY CHECK

We arrived at Gorakhpur and were allocated a government residence. This Type-IV flat featured two bedrooms, a lounge, and a guest room with an attached toilet, bathroom, and a veranda that connected the two bedrooms. The three of us—Abhay Ji, Ajay Ji, and I—were enrolled at the Government Inter College. According to regulations, government colleges were required to accept us as part of the agreement, thus allowing government officers to be relocated anytime during the year, thereby minimising the impact on their families. Only three months remained until the Final examinations for me in Class Ten and for Abhay Ji and Ajay Ji in Class Twelve.

The UP Board conducted both examinations at the state level, and all schools used the same question papers. Different examination centres evaluated the answer sheets to ensure uniform assessment across the state. Back at ASA College in Etah, the syllabus was only half complete, while at GIC Gorakhpur, teachers were revising all the subjects that were covered over the last two years. For the High School Boards, the subjects from Classes Nine and Ten would be included, and for the Intermediate Boards, the subjects from Classes Eleven and Twelve would be covered. This made these examinations extremely challenging, as tracking the content learned over the past two years was difficult.

On my first day in school, I sat in the middle of the back bench. Most of the students in this class had studied together for the last two years while I was new. The Maths teacher was testing the preparation of students:

"What is the formula for the Area of a Sphere?" the teacher asked a student on the front bench. The student got up from his chair and looked at the teacher as if he had not understood the question. As a courtesy, students must stand while responding to the teachers.

"Area of a Sphere?" Repeated the teacher. Still no response after another ten seconds.

Bang. The teacher slapped the boy with full power and shouted, "Four Pi R Square!"

My hand went straight to my left cheek as if the teacher had hit me. I did not know the answer.

"What the hell will you people do in the exams if you cannot answer such a basic question?" The teacher was so furious that he walked out of the class, leaving us alone to assess ourselves. The rest of the day at school was equally confusing. Different subject teachers were asking questions, and I was clueless.

I had no one to ask for help. The school was not going to be of any assistance. I was sure to fail. I knew I was downhill, but could I escape this hole? I started studying on my own. I occupied the guest room. It had space for a single bed and a study table. After returning from school, I drowned myself in textbooks till late at night. My elder brother Abhay Ji was keeping a close eye on me, and one day, he asked if he could join me. This provided me with additional encouragement.

The study table was big enough for two people. Sometimes, we slept just before our father got up around 4:00 am. Before going to sleep, I scribbled points on all the subjects that I had studied during the day without referring to any book. After my daily routine, I would attempt to recall all the bullet points which I had noted the previous night without consulting my notes. Every few days, I mentally reviewed the material and revisited the difficult topics. The routine continued for the next three months until the exams. Apart from meals, we were stuck in our room and were not visible to anyone at home.

In Science and Biology, 20% of marks were for practical exams. Traditionally, the internal teacher recommended the outstanding students to the external examiner, thus ensuring that they receive high marks, regardless of their performance. As my results would not count towards the results of this school, the teachers had no interest in me. This meant that I would just get passing marks in the practical exams regardless of my performance, thereby affecting my overall scores.

For the Science practical, I waited for the examiner to call me for Viva after completing my practical assignment, but it never happened. This was a sign of disaster. Two days later, I was due for the Biology practical. I did not want to take a chance. The examiner was a renowned Biology teacher and the author of high school and intermediate text books.

Soon after completing my practical assignment, I contacted the examiner and introduced myself. I asked him to review my assignment and clarify any questions about my knowledge. I mentioned that having transferred mid-session, the teacher was unaware of my background. The examiner looked at me and noted my name but did not ask any question or visit my practical assignment.

During the examination, I was under tremendous pressure and in a hurry to answer all the questions to avoid a low score. My handwriting reflected my speed and was not the best. I was confident that, in most cases, I had understood the question and was on the right track. However, I rarely had the chance to review my answers. A month later, the results were published in the newspaper, but my roll number was missing. This indicated that I had failed, but I assured my father that there must be something wrong, which could be due to the mix-up caused by our transfer.

My father took a two-day leave from his office to go to Allahabad to visit the UP Board headquarters. On return, my father scared me with the bad news that I did not do well in the Science practical. As it was essential to qualify the practical exam, there was no process to appeal against it. Nothing could be done now. I was staring at my father in disbelief. My father kept looking at me and then broke the silence.

"You have been given just passing marks, 8 out of 20 in the Science practical, but you have 18 out of 20 in Biology practical. Your total score is 352 out of 500. You have passed in first division. Your results were withheld as the marks for the practical exams did not arrive on time." My father told me in a somewhat flat tone.

He was disappointed with my performance. He expected me

to be on the Merit List. He asked me to work hard to secure a place on the Merit List in the following intermediate UP Board exams. I was relaxed, though not happy with the overall results. Being on the Merit List was an unrealistic expectation. I had never considered myself worthy of it.

My elder brother Abhay Ji could not retain his first division in the Intermediate exam and had to be content with second division. Intermediate UP Board exams are extremely hard compared to the High School exams. Most people lose about eight to ten percent of their high school scores. The government has kept high school as its literacy criteria and want most students to score higher than this. However, to be at par at the national level for higher studies through various universities, one must be competitive and pass the Intermediate exams with appropriate comprehension.

When I joined the next class after the summer vacations, the teachers were keen to know everyone's scores. The students stood one by one from the left of the first row to introduce themselves and their overall scores. It was the turn of the third student from the left corner of the first row. I could barely hear his soft tone, but the teacher's reaction was loud and clear.

"Four hundred and twenty-four. So, Diptiman, you must be on the Merit List." The whole class was aware of it except for the teacher and me. The Merit List comprised of the top ten position-holder students in the state.

"I am ranked fourth." The boy replied in a composed posture. I was dumbstruck. I had never met a person who had scored a place on the Merit List. For me, those people must look like aliens and could be spotted from afar; however, I could not even differentiate if this boy was standing or still sitting on his chair. He was the shortest boy in the class. His hair was cut in a typical *Gurukul* style, all around 4mm long. He was dark-complexioned, unimpressive, and thin to the extent of being weak. He did not even tell his full name. Just Diptiman, what about the surname? Sitting next to him was his elder brother, who resembled him quite a lot but was taller with a better build. He had scored above 370 marks, probably passed with distinction, meaning over 75%.

By the time all the boys finished introducing themselves and declared their scores, I had counted more than fifteen boys out of about forty students with better scores than me. Two boys sat together in the left corner of the back row, where I was also hiding, scoring 404 each or 80.8%. *"What have I done to myself? Oh God, please save me from these predators.* My pride had melted away. I was dwarfed. This was reality check for me.

For the next two years, I did not slow down my studies at home, nor did my elder brother, Abhay Ji. We both developed a good friendship and fought for the same cause. None of us wished to live in destitution or compromise our way of life. We had experienced a better life in Etah, where my father had served as Head of the Agriculture Department. We had developed pride in ourselves. Abhay Ji joined Gorakhpur University, opting for Zoology and Botany as his major subjects. My elder brother, Ajay Ji, suggested that I become a Mechanical Engineer to quench my curiosity since my questions were never-ending: "What makes an aeroplane fly? How could a ship carry so much weight and still float? I knew apples came from the tree, but where did pins and nails come from? How could a car start and run at such a speed?"

Ajay Ji told me that IIT produces the best engineers. My father also wanted me to become an engineer, but a Civil Engineer, and that too from Roorkee University, from where my Naresh uncle had graduated. He had many stories about Roorkee University and its prestige and how students must behave and dress in official attire for dinner. Though Roorkee University had its reputation in the past, the new norm was IIT (Indian Institutes of Technology). There were only five IITs in the country, one each in Kanpur, Delhi, Bombay, Madras, and Kharagpur. To become an engineer, I had to opt for Mathematics instead of Biology in Intermediate.

The competition in my class was intense, and no student helped the other boys. No one even smiled in the classroom, as if this would dilute their concentration and lead to a lack of understanding of the subject. Often, I made fun of things and cracked jokes to break the ice among the boys competing for the top rank. I was convinced that I would be ranked below fifteenth no matter what I did.

I developed a keen appreciation of Physics and was Mr Kaptan Yadav's favourite student. He always smiled mysteriously and challenged students with tricky questions. Most of the time, when all the students failed to respond, he would look at me and say, "Ultimately, I must ask you, Mr Johari." This was the understanding between us: even if I knew the answer, I would not raise my hand or reply unless all other options had been exhausted.

My father was transferred to Lucknow. About five months remained before my Intermediate UP Board Final exams. This time, my father was not keen to shift me or Abhay Ji to Lucknow due to the bad experience from the earlier transfer. Soon after finishing my Intermediate UP Board Final exams, I packed my bags and joined my parents in Lucknow. The IIT entrance exams were just 23 days away, and I had already lost one day due to packing and the journey to Lucknow. It was always a good idea to join coaching classes for preparation, but I had no time to research. I purchased the most popular guide for this exam, Arun's Guide, and went through it from A to Z.

In this guide, any question which had a footnote indicated that this was from one of the earlier IIT entrance exams which I had little difficulty in solving. I noticed that most of the questions from the earlier IIT entrance exams were unique, which meant they were not from prescribed textbooks and always contained a twist that was not covered in regular classes. Is this what made this entrance exam so tricky, specifically for students of UP Board?

Due to family pressure, I was also going to sit for the entrance exams for Roorkee, but I found it challenging to solve questions that had previously appeared in its entrance exam from the same Arun's Guide. Such questions aligned more with the syllabus and style of questions for the UP Board. For the next 22 days, I was stuck to a cot, which was my study table and the place to sleep. As expected, I did not do well in the Roorkee Entrance exams but was happy with my performance in the IIT Entrance exams, which were called the JEE, Joint Entrance Exams.

When the results of the IIT entrance exams were declared in the newspaper, I was in Kanpur with an elder cousin brother, Jyoti

Dada. He was completing his medical studies at Kanpur Medical College. I had come there to spend a week during the summer holidays. He called me:

"Atul, what's your Roll Number? The results for the IIT entrance exams are out."

Though I was awake, I was still in bed. I jumped out, sat beside him, and started scrolling the roll numbers. They were in ascending order. The rank was in brackets next to the roll numbers. My heart was filled with joy as I found my Roll Number listed, though the very next moment, it got settled. I noticed the numbers in the brackets: One, One, Nine, and Six. This was my rank out of some eighteen hundred selected candidates.

The next day, I returned to Lucknow to give the good news to my parents. Everyone was thrilled with my achievement. A few days later, the results of the Roorkee entrance examinations were declared. I was not selected. This disappointed my father somewhat, but I would be an engineer anyway so he was satisfied. My orientation programme was at IIT-Kanpur. I went there with my father. The faculty at IIT-Kanpur helped us in filling our preferences.

"You will not get any mainstream engineering, like mechanical, electrical, or electronic, in any of the IITs, but you will get the choice of your branch in BHUIT." Informed the Coordinating Officer.

"What is BHUIT?" I was confused about what BHUIT had to do with IIT.

"Institute of Technology in Banaras Hindu University. It is one of India's oldest engineering colleges within the Banaras Hindu University campus. A few years back, it joined hands with IIT for the combined entrance examination. Since then, the competition has been called JEE, the Joint Entrance Examination for all five IIT and BHUIT. It is a great institute, and you will not be disappointed. Make up your mind." Explained the Coordinating Officer.

I submitted for Mechanical Engineering at BHU as my first choice, followed by other streams at IITs Kanpur, Delhi, and Bombay. I also went through an essential medical examination, which we were told was only a formality and had no impact on the selection process. A few days later, I got confirmation from BHU that I had been allocated Mechanical Engineering. I had to join in the first week of July.

My UP Board Intermediate results were out. I had passed in first division. Once again, Diptiman was listed on the Merit List at fourth rank, the same as in high school. I exclaimed in amazement, how consistent was this boy? A few days later, I received my mark sheet by post. Three hundred and fifty out of five hundred. I was short by two numbers from my high school score. I expected a better score but was not too worried as my entry to engineering college through JEE was the ultimate milestone. A couple of weeks were still left to join BHUIT, and I was sitting on my cot one day when my mother approached me. She was looking a bit sad.

"So, you will leave us, Atul." She spoke softly, looking into my eyes. She had tears in her eyes. I had never looked at my achievements from this perspective. Now, I knew that every stick had two ends. Being the youngest, I was the most attached to my mother. Though I was the tallest in my family, I would still behave like an infant in front of her. I left no opportunity of sleeping with my mother, holding her tight in my arms as if someone would take her away from me. She was the safest place on earth for me. Though I loved and appreciated my father equally, it was always mixed with a touch of fear, so it was hard to enjoy the same closeness with him.

"Maa, I am just going for studies and will visit you every vacation." I consoled her with a tone of excitement while hiding my pain of separation. I had not yet realised that after this, I would never return to stay permanently with my parents. I was destined to leave the safest place on the planet. This is the rule of nature that all animals understand, except for human beings.

11. BHUIT

In July 1979, I reached Banaras with my father. I was on my way to BHUIT. The city was not as modern-looking as Lucknow until we reached the gates of Banaras Hindu University. As we entered the gate, I witnessed a total transformation in the surroundings. It seemed like we had entered a new world. *"Wow! This place is heaven."* Wide, one-way roads adorned with beautiful ornamental trees, and lined with flowers on either side along with a broad divider in between, that was filled with various shrubs and flowers. The architecture of the buildings proudly boasted the grace and solidarity of the Hindu culture. For the first time in my life, I felt proud to be a Hindu. Our destination was yet another kilometre and a half away.

On one side of the road were large buildings which were constructed with orange bricks. These buildings were student hostels. The other side of the street had even more grand and elegant buildings that were designated for various faculties. I was thrilled and excited with the surroundings, and any grudge for not getting into one of the IITs dissipated. My father told me that Mahamana Madan Mohan Malviya Ji had established this university through donations. Great people with enormous courage and vision sacrificed their lives to build a better society.

I was allocated a shared room in the Rajputana Hostel. Senior students helped us in locating our room and ensured that we were comfortable. They explained that each hostel had three to four messes which catered to the food requirements. These were run by the students and provided breakfast, lunch, evening tea, and dinner. The monthly bill would be about Rupees hundred and twenty-five. This was very reasonable.

The hostel was a square-shaped double-storey building with one big entrance. In the central was a large ground with lush green grass. All the rooms faced the centre ground. All around, a veranda connected all the rooms. Shared toilets and bathrooms could be found in each corner. The mess hall was at the ground level and had place for four different kitchens. Each hostel had another hall for gaming activities which mostly had Table Tennis. The institute was about half a kilometre away from the hostel. My father stayed overnight with me in the same hostel. He departed the next day. He looked very pleased with the facilities and the environment.

In the next few weeks, I went through mixed experiences. Senior students would come to our hostels at night with the intention of ragging. The drill started where we had to transform ourselves into Phantom, the famous comic character. We had to wear our underwear and vest over our trousers and shirt. I was very fond of these comic books. The characters Phantom, Mandrake, Lothar, and Hojo had a special place in my imagination, but I had never thought of impersonating Phantom in such an idiotic way.

Then, we had to entertain the seniors with jokes. I knew a few jokes, but these would not qualify as they had to be dirty jokes. Then we had to loudly and clearly repeat the swearing, as if we were going to war. We had to memorise the IT Anthem, a song that no one would dare utter in a social place. The only good thing was that stripping and slapping were prohibited. They could torture us mentally but not physically. One of the nicer senior students told me secretly that if I wanted to avoid any trouble then I should remember that I had no girlfriend, no sister, and no knowledge of any young female whatsoever.

Fresher's Night was due just a week before the first class tests, after which the senior students would leave us alone. The idea behind this whole exercise was to develop a bond with the senior students and, hopefully, find a mentor to help us with our studies and overcome homesickness. However, I failed in all these objectives.

The first test results were disastrous. No A-grade in any subject. I got a D in Technical English Writing, which meant that I had just passed. The overall score was 7.11 out of 10. I developed a complex. Was my selection to JEE just a fluke? Most of the students were fluent in English. They moved in small groups with boys from the same state who spoke the same mother tongue. The facial features of each student were so different that it looked almost impossible to identify them. The number of human species in India was baffling.

In all these different species I found one familiar face, Diptiman. He had also joined BHUIT in Electrical Engineering. Through him, I learned about our other batchmates from Intermediate. Out of the top fifteen students, we were the only two who had qualified for JEE. Others had been selected for Roorkee Engineering College or the combined entrance examination for all the regional Engineering colleges in the state. Some had been selected in both Roorkee and Regional Engineering colleges. In total, there were about twenty-three selections among these top students. This had never happened in the history of Government Jubilee College Gorakhpur.

Unfortunately, this history was never repeated again. Diptiman told me that he was sick during the JEE and thus could not perform well. As a result, his rank was similar to mine and therefore he preferred to come to BHUIT. Another reason Diptiman had chosen BHUIT was that his extended family lived in Banaras.

It was quite a challenge for me to adopt to the semester system as compared to yearly exams. Each year was divided into two independent semesters. Each semester had a mid-semester exam with 30% weightage, two class tests each with 10% weightage, and a final semester exam with 50% weightage. At times, the class tests were taken without prior notice.

Soon after the first semester, I was allocated a separate room. For the first four semesters, most engineering streams had somewhat similar syllabi, which must be why the allocation of hostels was not linked to the engineering branch for the initial two years. I remained in the Rajputana Hostel for the first two years. The more I focused on the books recommended by the syllabus, the worst I performed in the exams.

One day, a bright student disclosed a secret that all the test and exam questions were based on what was covered in the lessons, and to achieve good scores, one must attend all the classes and take thorough notes. By this time, I was through with three semesters, and enough damage had been done. For another two semesters, I tested this philosophy, and my grades improved each subsequent semester until, in the sixth semester, I decided to test my real potential.

I was in Vishwakarma Hostel with all mechanical, electrical, and civil engineering students from the third year. Each hostel could accommodate about 150 students. This semester, I took good notes in class and consistently referred to textbooks in the hostel during my spare time. My confidence was building slowly but steadily. When I received the grades for this semester, it was a bit of a disappointment: 8.7 out of 10.

I was sitting outside my room in a state of dejection when other students started discussing their scores. Most students swore and talked about the conspiracy theories by lecturers and professors. They must have decided to teach us a lesson that it was not all rosy, and, the Mechanical Engineering students should focus on their studies. It was a popular belief that Mechanical Engineering was the most effortless stream, and those who had done good *Karmas* in their past life were bestowed with Mechanical Engineering in BHUIT. This semester had proved it wrong.

Unlike past semesters, no student had scored a perfect 10. The highest grade was nine point something. Fifty percent of the students had got a Back in one or two subjects. My score was among the top ten students. That evening, I went to the Vishwanath Temple on the BHU campus to thank God, who had saved me from shame by giving me timely wisdom. What would my father have thought about me if I had got a Back in any subject?

The food in the Hostel Mess was phenomenal. For breakfast, there was milk, bread, and omelette. Those who did not like omelettes could opt for butter. Lunch consisted of fresh vegetables, lentils, and *chapatis*. Those who did not like seasonal vegetables had the choice of potatoes. Evening Tea had popular sweets and snack food. I was very fond of Samosas and would exchange my sweets with two Samosas with any willing fellow. I would then top it up with two extra Samosas and request the cook to scramble all six Samosas with fried onions as a dish for my evening tea.

Dinner was mostly fun food. One day, it could be stuffed Parathas, another day *Dosas*, yet another day, *Chole Bhature*. The dinner on Saturday was a feast. It was equivalent to a two-and-a-half-meal in terms of cost. Vegetarian people would get a *Paneer* dish and sweets, while the non-vegetarian people would get a quarter of chicken with curry. There were no evening tea and dinner on Sunday to compensate for the additional one-and-a-half towards the Saturday feast. This provided a much-needed break to the cook and the kitchen staff.

Our institute also had a Cafeteria that served food and snacks at subsidised rates. Here as well, my favourite was Samosa, which cost just Fifteen Paise. The locality just outside the main gate of BHU was called Lanka. The sweet shop in one of the corners was a favourite spot among students where *Long Lata*, the most exotic and fulfilling sweet dish, was served for Rupee one each. The closest description of Long Lata is milk-cake wrapped in flour, coiled to form about two and a half circles, dip-fried and served hot after dipping in a somewhat thick, warm sugar syrup.

One Long Lata and you were done for the rest of the day, especially for students who would skilfully avoid paying and escape silently from the shop after devouring it to their complete satisfaction. Some students had also developed the habit of bunking the Saturday feast and instead enjoyed a movie with light snacks or somewhat cheaper food within Banaras city. Mostly students maintained a push bike to commute to the city. Despite such tasty and healthy food, most students did not gain weight, and I too, remained thin, weighing just over fifty kilograms.

Apart from studies, there was a whole plethora of extracurricular activities. Among cultural activities, competitions were held at the hostel and institute levels for Dumb Charades, What's the Good Word, Jest a Minute, Elocution, Debate, Creative Writing, Singing, Instrumental Music, Plays, and Skits. Some of these activities were also conducted in Hindi in honour of being a part of the Hindu University, though these activities were not as popular as their English counterparts.

In sports, there were Table Tennis, Carrom, and Chess. Athletic activities included short and long races and a 10-km walk. The BHU campus also had a swimming pool, a gym, and a flying club. The foreign language faculty offered part-time diplomas in French and German languages.

I had brought Banjo and Harmonica from home when I joined BHUIT. These were my new hobbies. Before joining BHUIT, when we were in Gorakhpur, my brother Abhay Ji bought a Banjo after listening to a mesmerising musical performance by three brothers at their residence during our visit. After two days of hard work, Abhay Ji realised that what looked like a piece of cake was not that easy. Often, we become so engrossed in the effortless performances of the artists that we fail to recognise the immense effort that goes into making them appear effortless.

In two days, he could only get the first twelve notes of the title song from the movie *Kora Kagaj*. Once he discarded this defective instrument, it was my turn to test it. Either it was a miracle, or the Banjo did not want to stretch its luck further. I got the first two main lines of the song within half an hour. By another day, I could play the whole song, though not fluently.

I had found a new friend. I knew I had some connections with music, but I was still uncertain if it would articulate. When I was young, three distant cousin sisters visited us in Lucknow. Whenever they picked up the *Harmonium* or the *Dholak* (a percussion instrument) to sing folk songs, I would fall asleep in no time, irrespective of the time of day. This happened at least three times in three days. I was amazed by the power of music as I rarely slept during the daytime.

After my success with the Banjo, I tried the Harmonica which we had purchased during our trip to the Nepal border from Gorakhpur. Once again, it did not disappoint me. When Diptiman and I were in the same hostel during my third year of engineering, he would come to my room to learn the Banjo. He also borrowed it for a week and returned it after he purchased a new one.

The keys on his Banjo resembled those on a keyboard, unlike the buttons on my Banjo, which made it somewhat easier to play. Within a few weeks, Diptiman mastered a few songs and participated in the Solo Instrumental Music category along with me. Diptiman came first for his performance of "*Tu Ganga ki Mauj Mai Jamuna ki Dhara...*", a song from a classic Indian movie. He skilfully played every delicate note along with the filler music and won the hearts of the judges and audience alike. I was not even among the top three competitors.

Diptiman and I were concerned with the popularity and shortcomings of some of the events that were conducted in Hindi, specifically Jest a Minute and What's the Good Word. We decided to take things into our hands. At the beginning of the fourth year, Diptiman proposed his name as Secretary for all Hindi literary activities and was elected. He wanted me to take charge of the two activities for which he had already coined the names. *Shabdanjali* for What's the Good Word and *Chadikiyain* for Jest a Minute. These were beautiful titles. The rest was up to me.

I spent a lot of time going through Hindi dictionaries to make a list of interesting words and topics for the two games. I also consulted with professors from the Hindi faculty to fine-tune the rules of the games and the decision-making process so that it was fair to people from all the states. As several participants from Bihar state had different accents for some words, the dilemma was whether we should acknowledge their accents or insist on the correct accent.

Another challenge was identifying the words from a foreign language, especially Urdu, and finding the Hindi equivalent. My hard work paid off, and the popularity of these two games skyrocketed. Next year, in my final year of engineering, the *Kashi Yatra* festival, featuring cultural and literary activities from various institutions, was a crucial test to validate the rightful place for these activities. Over the week, every night, we also enjoyed exclusive performances by internationally renowned artists such as Ustad Bismillah Khan for *Shahnai*, Girja Devi for classical singing, and another famous *Kathakali* dancer.

I was in the final semester of the final year, and the air was hot with the hustle and bustle of campus recruitment. Every week, recruitment teams of big brand companies were busy with their selection processes. Most of the students had been preparing for their GRE, GMAT, and CAT (entrance exams for IIM) that would open doors for them in foreign universities or MBA (Master of Business Administration) within India. For such students, campus recruitment was just a backup option or a stopover for a few months. At an estimate, at that time, around 70% students from IIT and BHUIT left the country within two years of passing out.

I was among the remaining 30%, who were desperate to get a job. None of my elder brothers had secured a job yet, and I did not want to deprive my parents of their last hope. As a lonely planet, I did not know much about the GRE, GMAT, or CAT. In fact, by now, I was fed up with my studies and had realised that whatever we studied would not help us in the real world. My father wanted me to get into IAS (Indian Administrative Services), but I was well aware of my limitations. My goal was to secure a confirmed job offer.

The owner of the Hyderabad Asbestos and Cement Limited came for campus recruitment, but no one applied. It was a small company, and the job offer was not attractive. They were offering Rs 1100 per month as starting salary. The product Asbestos itself had a bad image. Everyone advised me not to apply for this company, but I did not want to miss an opportunity and appeared for the interview.

"Why have you applied for this job." Questioned the owner of the company.

"I want to secure a job. So far, I have no job in my hand." I replied honestly.

"I am offering you a job. Please ignore the salary that we have advertised. It will be much better than what we have announced. This is just the stipend we pay to our trainees. You will join us as an executive, and we also have a plant outside India that you might end up looking after. Can you confirm that you will join us?" Explained the owner.

"If I cannot secure any other job, I will join your company," I replied thankfully.

I now had a confirmed job, though my friends were upset that I had wasted one choice.

I kept applying for other campus recruitment offers to improve the offer that I had, but it looked like the recruiters had specific criteria for selection. This could be based on your hometown, surname, or response style, and not your performance. Irrespective of this, if I got to the interview stage, I did well as I could navigate the discussions towards my summer vacation project, which I had completed the previous year in Scooter's India Limited Lucknow, my hometown.

This was a six-week project, and the task was to get consistent fuel consumption for their new 100cc scooter, Cento, which the company wanted to launch as a fuel-efficient scooter. At the time, most scooters had 150cc engines and travelled about 35 to 45 km per litre. The target for this scooter was above 60km/litre. The issue was that the results were inconsistent from day to day, from lab to road tests, and from one scooter to another.

Mr Trivedi, the Senior Manager for this product, gave me a free hand to formulate and execute the strategies. He also introduced me to the Line Manager and Supervisor. The deadline was two months. Mr Trivedi had to produce a scooter for the approving authorities and get the certification before the final launch in the market. I had absolutely no clue how to tackle this issue. Still, the motivation was that if I could resolve the problem, I might get a job offer and be able to live with my parents for the rest of my life.

After multiple lab tests, Mr Trivedi was happy to find a scooter that consistently averaged above 70km/litre on the road, and he also found the root cause for fuel inconsistency. I spent another two weeks completing the project report, which included the exploded sketching of the various assemblies.

Unfortunately, Scooters India Limited Lucknow did not come for campus interviews. However, the work I did with them proved handy in impressing other interviewers. This year, Bharat Electronics Ghaziabad looked very impressive. I was interviewed and offered a provisional selection. Though they assured me that the provisional selection was as good as the final selection, theoretically, I still had the option of appearing in more campus recruitments.

I was scheduled for an interview with Bharat Pump and Compressor Limited, a state public sector company in Allahabad. If I could not find a job in Lucknow, my second option was Allahabad, which is closer to Lucknow. As soon as I entered the room, one of the two interviewers left without even acknowledging me. The second one asked me to take a seat and questioned:

"What type of job do you want to do?" It was a direct question.

"I do not know, but you can help me. I will be unable to do a repetitive job and will get bored. I need to have new challenges." I exposed my weakness.

"Process Engineering will be the right type of job for you." Replied the interviewer.

"What is Process Engineering." I could not hide my curiosity or ignorance.

The interviewer picked up the little manual bell that is usually found at the reception of an office or shop to attract someone's attention. He then queried.

"Can you explain the process of manufacturing the top portion of this bell?"

I was not expecting a technical question, but I kept my composure and replied.

"You first punch the round piece from the flat metal sheet. During this process, a hole will also be punched in the centre to avoid an additional operation later. Then, it will be taken to the press to form a hollow semi-spherical shape." As I was explaining, the other interviewer returned and stood at the door. He interrupted in the colloquial Hindi language.

"*Chalal Jai.*" Meaning, let us go.

The interviewer stood up and walked out as if I was not there. Both vanished while I was still sitting in the room, confused. After waiting a few minutes, I realised it was lunchtime, and the interview was over.

A few days later, I had another interview. After a few questions, the interviewer doubted if I was a final-year Mechanical Engineering student and politely informed me:

"I can offer you a job if you tell me your current subjects for the semester."

I was blank. I had been so busy with extracurricular activities and campus interviews that I had lost touch with the classes. I tried to dodge the bullet.

"M510, S508." I was interrupted by the interviewer.

"Could you please share the detailed titles of your semester's subjects?" The interviewer smiled.

"I'm sorry. I cannot recall now. Thanks." I got up and walked out.

Although I had one confirmed and one provisional offer, they were valid only if I completed my Mechanical Engineering that year. This was a challenging task. I had never felt so out of place. I was terrified. Luckily, I passed my final semester with a reasonable grade, but the experience affected me so severely that for the next ten years, I suffered frequent nightmares and would wake up at night drenched in sweat. I would then assess my surroundings. This is Shalu, sleeping next to me. There is Manu, my son, and Ninni, my daughter. I am working as an Engineer at Bharat Electronics, Ghaziabad.

PART 3
THE COUPLE

12. THE BEGINNING

It was my last big holiday break with my parents. Once again, they were posted to Gorakhpur. I had finished my engineering and was waiting to join my job. I had appointment letters from Bharat Electronics Ghaziabad and Engineers India Limited through my campus recruitment. I also appeared in the NTPC (National Thermal Power Corporation) entrance exam to protect myself from being jobless. This was a large national public sector, and by some luck, I was selected for it.

One day, my sister, Renuka, who had come from Gauhati to spend time with us, brought a letter to me and said, "This is for you. It has your name on it." As I opened it, I started laughing in disbelief. It was an appointment letter from Bharat Pumps and Compressors Limited Allahabad. I told the story of my interview to the whole family. How one after the other, both interviewers had walked out of the room, leaving me alone, wondering about the outcome.

I had also appeared in GATE, the combined entrance exams for M Tech (Master of Technology) for all IITs, to stick around for studies, if I failed to secure a job. However, I was disqualified due to poor performance. The letter used very polite language, stating that I was free to appear again next year.

Choosing between EIL (Engineers India Limited) and BE (Bharat Electronics) was difficult. EIL was a well-established and prestigious company that carried out large infrastructure projects throughout India and neighbouring countries, while BE Ghaziabad was a relatively new company. The name BE suggested that it was mainly for electronics stream, and engineers from other branches would have limited prospects. However, the salary and the designation looked much more attractive.

Another significant advantage was that Ghaziabad district was part of Uttar Pradesh, sharing the borders with the capital of India, New Delhi. My father wanted me to prepare for IAS (Indian Administrative Services), India's most prestigious government job. However, I was aware of my shortcomings. I kept making excuses which upset him. The harder my father tried to convince me, the worse my arguments became, thus leaving a bad taste in his mouth. Our relationship soured, but my limitations and arrogance became my best friends. My father's best hopes had shattered but I knew that I had lost all my energy halfway through my journey. After getting into IIT/JEE, I had become an average student, who was scared of studies and was content with my limitations.

I joined BE Ghaziabad and rented a one-room set that was built on the first floor of a reasonably big house in Kavi Nagar. A company bus picked me up daily about fifty metres from my residence. The factory was about half an hour's drive, in Sahibabad, an industrial area just near the border of New Delhi. My landlord was helpful and did not interfere much. As there was no other construction on the first floor, I had a full terrace and did not feel jailed in my one-room set. I equipped my little kitchen and often cooked for myself. The food in restaurants was spicy, which upset my stomach. The factory timings were from 8:30 am to 5:00 pm.

There were thirteen people in our batch, who had all been selected through campus recruitments from various prestigious institutions, like IIT Delhi and Kanpur, BHUIT, XLRI Jamshedpur and NEETI Bombay. We went through a two-week orientation programme where heads of different departments explained their roles, facilities, and challenges. We were also given tours of the various departments. BE Ghaziabad had a vast campus of approximately 1 x 1.5 square kilometres. It featured four large manufacturing hangars with attached offices and a separate large building for Design and Engineering, in addition to the administrative building, warehouses, canteens, creche, and many more hi-tech specific purpose facilities.

The main product of BE Ghaziabad was Radars for the Indian Army. Due to the technology used to produce a Radar, the unit was a president's house regarding the latest technology. I was overwhelmed by the facility and the state-of-the-art technologies. The average age of executives was around twenty-seven, with about three hundred executives. The non-executive cadre had about two thousand employees with an average age of around thirty-five.

During the orientation tour, I was amazed by the air-conditioned hangar within the machine shop, where computerized machining centres automatically changed tools, managed coolant, adjusted cutting parameters, and followed precise cutting profiles. The operators stood by to load and unload the parts once the machine stopped and the yellow lights flashed.

"What is this section called?" I asked the operator.

"This is the CNC Machining Section. All these machines run on the programmes prepared by the NC Programming Cell. In this section, we have the Machining Centres and Turning Centres, but we also have an NC Turret Punch in the next hangar." Replied the operator proudly.

I made up my mind and expressed my choice of placement to the HR Manager. I told him that I had other job offers from prestigious companies but would not look elsewhere if I got a place in the NC Programming Cell. Luckily, another engineer of our batch, Kamarjit Singh and I were posted in this section. For the whole five years of engineering, I had only one subject in Computer Programming, which I had considered a waste of time. I had mugged five programmes, three of which had come in the exams, and I had passed it with a B grade. I was relieved that I would never have to deal with computers again. But life is full of surprises. It prepares you for something and tests you against another thing.

For the next few months, Kamarjit and I worked hard and went through the manuals to master the art of Programming. We upskilled ourselves in computer languages, BASIC, and other applications to make housekeeping programmes to ensure that we were not duplicating the programmes. We had a DOS-based computer with a MPM operating system. In simple words, this was one of the first desk computers by Microsoft which had multiple workstations that were connected to the same desk computer.

BASIC was a high-level computer language that was developed by Microsoft, through which powerful software could be developed. This was the time before MS Word and Excel were born. Word Master was a programme for limited document writing.

Impressed by our hard work and achievements, our manager

disclosed two computer games which were installed on this computer, and we enjoyed them thoroughly. So that we could play computer games within the enclosed computer room without interruptions from another Senior Engineer in our section, we developed a Programme that we ran on the third workstation. This simulated the command screen but responded differently to common commands and displayed error messages. As expected, this annoyed the Senior Programmer, who complained to our manager that his terminal did not function properly when these two Deputy Engineers were in the computer room. However, this could not be proven, and we continued to enjoy playing computer games in private.

One day, my cousin brother, Manoj Kudesia, came into our home. He had a job offer in Ghaziabad. He had completed Chemical Engineering from HBTI Kanpur, a three-year Degree course and was selected for this job through campus selection.

Manoj Ji was about two years older than me. I was not very friendly with him due to a brawl I had with him as a child. Though I have a poor memory and find it hard to remember things, I am equally bad at forgetting my differences with people. I suppose the difference between a friend and a relative is that you can choose to drop a friend but not a relative. I welcomed Manoj Ji and offered him to stay with us as long as he could not find a place to rent. However, I also warned him that it did not mean that he could take it easy and not try his best. He found a room nearby within a week and shifted there. During his stay with us, we both had a good time. This helped in improving our relationship, and we became friends.

At this time, my two elder brothers, Ajay Ji and Abhay Ji, were doing their higher studies at Lucknow University. They were living in hostels in the university campus. Sharad Ji, Shalu's elder brother, had come to Lucknow for some work and came across Ajay Ji. He mentioned he was looking for a suitable match for his sister, Shalini. Ajay Ji laughed and expressed his surprise.

"How come you are concerned about your sister's marriage? She was a tiny one when we were in Etah."

"Of course, Partner, she was in class five then, but now she is doing her BA final from Dayalbagh Degree College in Agra. It has been eight years since you were in Etah. Time flies, doesn't it?" Sharad Ji replied with his typical loud laughter.

"In that case, I have my younger brother, Atul. He has completed his engineering from BHU and works at Bharat Electronics Ghaziabad. If you want, I can give you his address so you can see him before you take it any further." Ajay Ji replied. Ajay Ji was a friend of friends and would offer anything in his possession in the name of friendship. He would go to any extent to help his friends. Abhay Ji and I often criticised his virtue by singing the song from the movie Zanjir, "*Yaari Hai Iman Mera Yaar Meri Zindagi…*" (Friend is my life and my soul). This movie had given Amitabh Bachchan, the biggest superstar of Bollywood, the title of Angry Young Man.

Sharad Ji and Pradeep Ji, elder brothers of Shalu, had graduated from Law and following the family tradition, practised in Etah. One fine Sunday morning, Sharad Ji visited me in Ghaziabad and introduced himself.

"Partner, I am Sharad Kumar, Advocate from Etah. You can probably recall me. I was your elder brother Ajay's class fellow and friend in ASA Inter College Etah. I got your address from him when I was in Lucknow last month. I was chatting with him about a suitable match for my younger sister, Shalini. He suggested you. Do you mind if I ask your opinion about marriage?" Asked Sharad Ji.

"Yes, I do have some recollection. Your face looks familiar. I am the youngest in my family, and none of my brothers are married yet. None of them are employed either, so the matrimonial process is out of the question for any of us. How can I think about marriage while my elder brothers remain unmarried?" I tried to close the matter.

"I understand, Partner; I am just trying to know your opinion about the girl you would consider as your life partner. Marriage is a long process. It can take more than a year to finalise the whole thing. What are your likings?" Sharad Ji was not ready to leave the ground.

"I have no liking, though if a girl has spent two years in a hostel, it would please me. I spent five years in a hostel for my engineering degree, which impacted me positively. Though, in our society, it is difficult for girls to live in hostels for higher studies, but if they get this opportunity, even if for only two years, it will help them to face the world. But I can assure you that this is not my demand, and I have decided that I will not reject any genuine proposal and will go ahead with the first proposal that comes my way.

If you are serious about your sister, contact my parents. That would be the proper channel. I am not entertaining any proposal directly." I replied in a somewhat firm and flat tone. I had nothing more to tell Sharad Ji. He had understood that there was no point in hanging around and departed after wishing me well.

After a few months, my parents contacted me and told me about Etah's marriage proposal. They also told me that the girl's brother is Ajay Ji's friend, and the family is well-known in Etah. They told me that If I wanted, they could come to my place and would go to Etah to meet the family and see the girl in person. I agreed.

This was the first time my parents would visit me in Ghaziabad. I was excited to show them my little establishment. My kitchen utensils, cutlery, a little gas stove mounted on a two-litre LPG gas cylinder and all bits and pieces. At that time, getting a proper gas connection was hard, so I had to compromise with this type of a gas stove. Due to its overall height and slenderness, it was a little unstable, and I had to be careful. I had a collection of lentils, rice, flour, spices, and other necessary things which were neatly stored in plastic bottles. Would I be able to impress my mother with my cooking skills? Would my father be proud to see me settling independently and doing well?

As far as marriage was concerned, my father had already clarified that he had no dowry demands. I wanted a simple marriage ceremony, ideally, a court marriage, if both the families would agree. My family members knew my intention of not rejecting any girl after meeting her, so this meeting was merely a formality, and consequently, the gathering would be pleasant. My father was also opposed to rejecting the proposal, as he had experienced the trauma of such rejections himself.

My parents, elder brother Abhay Ji and eldest brother Arun Ji arrived at my place. We had a good time. A couple of days before we had to leave for Etah, my mother stepped on an unstable patch of footpath. She suffered a hairline crack in her ankle and was restrained to the bed. We informed Sharad Ji about this accident and requested that their family and Shalini visit us in Ghaziabad. They agreed. Sharad Ji went to Agra to bring Shalu. She came to Etah but was furious with the idea of visiting us. She had witnessed the nuisance that her two aunties, the younger sisters of Suman aunty, had been through during the matrimonial process. She felt increasingly frustrated.

"These bloody idiot boys, what do they think of themselves? How can they reject a girl? Who has granted them this right? Why must we endure all the pain only to be told off?

"I am not going anywhere; they can come here to see me. How dare they interrupt my studies? They should also take some pain to have free tea, samosas, and sweets." Announced Shalu.

Everyone else had failed to persuade Shalu. It was her father's turn. Ravindra Kumar, who had never done anything against her wishes, got up from his place, walked slowly to come closer to Shalu, and hugged her.

"Lalli, you do not have to go anywhere if you do not want to. They had planned to come here, but maybe this was not God's wish. We will tell them to fix another date to come here to meet us." Ravindra Kumar placed his right palm over her head and moved it gently in an expression of love to comfort her, still hugging her softly. His eyes were wet as if they were saying, "I also cannot live without you. You are my lifeline."

That evening, everyone had dinner in silence. Only the noise of the cutlery and plates could be heard. Before going to bed, Shalu approached her parents to bid them good night but paused momentarily and spoke.

"I have already lost all this time. I will go to Ghaziabad tomorrow with you on the condition that no one tells me how to dress, how to behave, or what to do. This is the last time I will do this. Hopefully, I will get some sleep. Good night."

Shalu's mother's anger evaporated. Just a moment earlier, she had criticised her husband for being immature and incapable of adapting to the times and advising their children properly. However, it was all in a soft yet firm and nagging tone.

"You go along with Munnu and Raju. I must be here for my court hearing. All should go well. Do not worry much." Ravindra Kumar consoled his wife, Saroj.

The journey by any Roadways bus is never a pleasant experience, especially when you are on a special mission. They took a short break at their relative's place in Ghaziabad to freshen up before coming to our place. There had hardly been any conversation during the six-hour journey. After a brief refreshment and rest, the lady of the house, Vinod Mausi, who was the cousin sister of Shalu's mother, suggested that Shalu wash her face, apply light make-up, and comb her hair to remove the dust and dullness of the journey and change her dress to suit the occasion.

Shalu went to the washroom and changed her dress to a designer Green Silk suit, but instead of following all the other commands, she poured plenty of oil on her head and put a thick coat of oily cream on her face. This made her look like a village girl with little understanding of makeup. Her pointed shoes showed her completely out of fashion. This was done to remind everyone of the conditions of agreeing to this visit.

Any more instructions or persuasion would do more harm than good. On her way to our place, Shalu scratched her nail polish. Shalu's mother had been praying to all the gods. *"Oh God, please grant wisdom to my daughter. Please help her calm down. Please do not allow all our efforts to go waste."*

I received everyone just outside my room. Shalu was the last one in the row. We were face to face, just about a couple of feet away.

"Namaste." I greeted her with my hands joined in front of my chest in a typical textbook style. I received no response. Instead, I felt the heat of two laser beams coming from her eyes, piercing straight into mine. The message was loud and clear: *"Who are you? Get out of my way. Do not even think about messing with me."* I stepped aside to give her room. Shalu entered the room, glanced around, and folded her hands to greet everyone silently.

Everyone crammed into the room, and started chatting. My parents were trying to make everyone comfortable and thanked Shalu's family for their efforts in visiting us. As the conversation progressed, it became evident to Shalu that I was responsible for this situation. After about half an hour, my father asked me to prepare tea. I stood up to leave the room and head to the kitchen.

Shalu's mother subtly suggested that Shalu join me and take the initiative to make the tea. It was an indirect call for her to do so. Shalu ignored the prompting and did not move. I prepared the tea and was ready to bring it, but this time, Shalu's mother gave her daughter a direct command.

"Shalu, please go to the kitchen and help him in bringing the tea."

Now, Shalu had no choice and entered the kitchen. She was tall and slender, with larger-than-average eyes and perfectly aligned teeth. She stood upright and confident, showing no signs of embarrassment or discomfort.

"My mom has sent me to get the tea. Where can I find the tray?" Asked Shalu.

"Sorry, I do not have a tray. I will bring it myself. You do not have to worry," I replied, and thankfully she returned empty-handed to the room.

I brought everything and placed it on the small folding table. Shalu's mother asked Shalu once more.

"At least pour the tea and serve it to everyone."

Shalu tried to pour the tea into the first cup, but it was not the best pour and spilt onto the plate.

"Leave it to me. It is a bit tricky to pour from this kettle. The lid must be left a little open to avoid spilling." I rescued Shalu and served tea to everyone.

As the conversations continued, I stepped out of the room, went to the edge of the terrace, and leaned against the rails. Within five minutes, my elder brother Abhay Ji joined me. He had been remarkably observant and had sensed my state of confusion. He spoke to me in a very gentle manner.

"You do not have to say anything. I will reject this proposal to keep you out of trouble."

"That would not be correct. Even if you reject the proposal, I will be responsible for this. I will stick to my decision. I cannot say no. I will not say no," I said firmly. All the clouds had gone. My mind was clear. I had decided. I would not disappoint myself. Abhay Ji stayed beside me for a few minutes and then returned to the room. I followed him after about another five minutes.

My father was chatting with Shalu, trying to learn more about her. "What are your hobbies? What were your subjects in high school and intermediate school? What was your score in different subjects? How is your experience in the hostel so far? Do you still get homesick?" I suddenly interrupted my father and suggested:

"Papa Ji, ask her some things that will be relevant in life." I believed that all these schools, colleges, and universities were not particularly helpful in confronting the real challenges of life. They aimed to make a person a jack of all trades but master of none. To excel in life, one needed to be king in at least one area, which might not be related to the subjects that are studied. Before my father could respond to me, Shalu's mother handed over the ball to me:

"Why don't you ask her anything that you need to know?" All eyes were focused on me. Shalu was staring at me as if saying, *"Come on, show me your true colour now, and I will give you the knowledge you need for the rest of your life."*

"Do you know cooking?" My question was brief but pivotal for a happy family life. I had seen the pain and love with which my mother prepared meals for us every day, six times a day. I saw food as something that brought us all together. It is the source of all our emotions and helps us in building our personality. It is food that cultivates friendships. It is food that determines our health. If there is insufficient food, you share with others so no one is hungry. If there is more food, you preserve it like the most precious thing that will save you in hard times. Food is not something you buy. Food is something you prepare for someone you care about and love.

Everyone was shocked at my question. Out of all the things on earth, I had chosen to ask about cooking. Does everyone marry to get a chef? Shalu's mother was feeling guilty about why she had not forced her daughter to learn cooking. Whenever she tried to take her to the kitchen, Shalu's father would object, "Don't torture my little girl." Shalu's elder brother, Sharad Ji, went cold, but her eldest brother, Pradeep Ji, had his back towards me but was facing Shalu. He had a cheeky smile to encourage her to use her intellect and come up with a brilliant response.

"I do know cooking." This was Shalu's verbal response, but she delivered it angrily after taking my full scan, which communicated a lot more to me. *"You dumb boy, don't you know that every girl knows cooking, and so do I?"* I was bruised by the sharp response, trying to hide my pain and took time to recover. Shalu had realised my situation and decided to deliver the second fatal blow and establish herself the winner.

"It will be edible for you. At least." Another precise, well-executed move like a ten-degree Taekwondo Black belter. She had an expression of satisfaction on her face, but her eyes were still focused on me as if asking, "*Do you need more?*" Shalu's eldest brother, Pradeep Ji, clasped his palms tightly to avoid clapping on the brilliant answer. He had trained her well. He was clever and worldly wise. He was the one who had insisted that Shalu should do her higher education away from Etah, from a reputed university, and live in a hostel to face life first-hand. He had shared the winning formula with her. Face the fear.

"No problems at all. Even if you do not know, I will teach you." I answered politely. This was to clarify that this was not a condition for settlement. To me, it really did not matter what one knew but it mattered what one was prepared to learn. Everyone was laughing at the end of our brief duel. No one was hurt.

"Atul, could you please get Rupees hundred from my wallet for Shalini? I want her to buy chocolates for herself." My father delivered the message. Shalu had won me over. My mother appeared happy and satisfied. My eldest brother, Arun Ji, smiled and could not hide his joy. Abhay Ji shook his head, wondering if I realised the gravity of the situation and if I could stand firm under the challenging conditions in this relationship. Shalu's mother looked at everyone in disbelief. Sharad Ji was relaxed. Pradeep Ji was delighted. Shalu was baffled, thinking, *"What sort of boy is this? Why has he not retaliated at any of my misbehaviour?"*

All the conversations had finished. Everyone looked relaxed and happy. It was time for the final departing greeting. Shalu was the last to come out of the room, standing at a distance, waiting for others to go downstairs. I used this opportunity to come closer and stand beside her. I noticed tiny flakes of white paint had fallen from the ceiling onto her hair. I spoke softly so only Shalu could hear.

"Some white paint flakes have fallen onto your head from the ceiling. You will need to remove them. Just remember, you do not need to stress any longer. You are mine now. Have fun." Shalu did not reply. She did not even turn her face towards me to avoid making it evident that we were having some conversation. Maybe she was still in a state of shock and was completely unaware of her surroundings.

Back at Vinod mausi's house, the confusion prevailed amid joy. Questions were coming from everywhere: *"How can this possibly happen? Did Shalu change her mood and behaviour? What were their demands? Does the boy have some serious flaws? What do you know about his family? What does he look like? Does he have two eyes and speak without stammering? What is his education? What is his age? What is his height? What is his complexion? Does he walk straight?"*

Back in Etah, Shalu's mother was unable to control her emotions. All the other family members gathered around her, though it was late at night. The commentary was on, and the actions were being replayed:

"Why was Shalu's marriage settled while her father was still in Etah? You told us that you had to see your cousin sister as she was not well." Raj aunty asked.

"But we just went to see the boy. This was our first visit for her marriage settlement. There was no point in saying anything unless the marriage was settled. It just makes the girl sad." Countered Saroj Ji.

Amid this chaos, Shalu's father hugged her and asked:

"Lalli, did you like the boy?"

"No." Replied Shalu. Though she meant yes, she was shy.

"Why not?" Asked her dad.

"He has hazel eyes and a brown moustache." Shalu hugged her father with love.

"Is that a problem?" Asked Ravindra Kumar.

"Not really, but how dare he ask me if I know cooking." This time, Shalu looked cheerfully, directly into his eyes, as if she was saying, *"I have no complaints. I am fine. I am still trying to get the hang of it."*

Sharad Ji stood proudly before his father. His chest was inflated at least four inches. Pradeep Ji could hardly contain his smile. The next day, Shalu returned to Agra, as her BA Final exams were merely a month away, and she did not wish to waste any more time. Pradeep Ji had postponed his decision to move to Allahabad High Court and opted to remain in Etah until her marriage, thus allowing him to spend more time with Shalu. There was much to prepare in the lead-up to the wedding. If Jagrani, Shalu's grandmother, were still alive today, she would have been delighted to learn that Shalu's husband was fairer and taller than her son-in-law, Jagdish.

13. THE MARRIAGE

After Shalu finished her BA Final exams, she returned to Etah and enrolled for MA in History as a private student, as advised by Bhaiya uncle. Soon after she arrived at Parmesh Sadan, she got sick and was diagnosed with typhoid fever. This lasted for over two months, and she became very weak. I informed my parents of this and expressed my intention to visit her. My parents expressed that they would also join me at Etah. I reached a day in advance. I brought a selection of chocolates for Shalu. I also prepared an audio cassette of my favourite songs to please her.

My parents were delighted with the hospitality of Shalu's mother. They left the next day. But I stayed one more day. This was a pleasant change for Shalu. She had witnessed a child within me. She also noticed our closeness and was assured that she would fit well into our family. Her fever came under control within the next two weeks, but it took a few more weeks for her to recover completely.

Later, she told me that she had been stealing mangoes from the big basket. She was advised to adhere to a strict diet but could not resist the temptation of mangoes. But after we left Etah, she followed the recommended diet and thus got well. Shalu and I kept in touch through letters. Her Urdu *Sher O Shayari* (poetry) overwhelmed me. I responded to some extent with my Hindi poems. We shared our favourite song titles to convey our emotions and indulged in a little romance.

My marriage settlement was a good start for my family. My father was also trying to find a suitable match for my eldest brother. It was a difficult task as he did not have any job and also suffered from depression. Finally, he found a girl, and they were married. Unfortunately, the marriage lasted only a few months, though to my surprise, Dada took it bravely and was not impacted much by the breakup.

Within the same year, my father settled a match for Ajay Ji as well. The wedding date was set for December 1985, two days before my wedding. Abhay Ji was completing his PhD while preparing for the IAS exams, and he did not need any distractions. In October, on my birthday, we had a little ceremony at my parents' residence in Gorakhpur to fix this match. Shalu came to our place with her parents and relatives. They stayed in our house for one night and two days. As Shalu was a Sitar student, we bought a brand-new Sitar to enjoy her performance. The stay was enjoyable.

In Etah, preparations had started for my marriage. Partial advance payments were made to the band, cooks, florists, and tents. Everyone in Parmesh Sadan was excited. After over thirty years, Parmesh Sadan would be decorated again for a marriage ceremony. Before this, Shalu's Bua, aunty Shail's marriage was performed there. The glory of that marriage had not yet faded from people's memories.

As mentioned, Shalu and I exchanged letters. She took private tuition for Urdu from a Maulvi Ji, who visited her weekly at Parmesh Sadan. Shalu wanted to refine her poetry writing. Sher O Shayari is a specific style of poetry in Urdu that communicates a profound and passionate messages within two lines. She teased me with her Sher O Shayari through the letters. There would be at least three to four difficult words in each *Sher* that I had no clue about. It was a thrill for Shalu to jumble these newly learned words into somewhat meaningful arrangements.

There was a Muslim employee in my office at the NC Programming Cell, Jarar Husain, whom I consulted to decode these words. Usually, he insisted on knowing the whole sentence. He argued that the meaning of each word could change depending on its use, but I wanted to keep our love affair a secret. Everyone else in our office enjoyed this tug-of-war between him and me, hoping to get some nectar out of it.

The next week, there was a Public Holiday on Saturday. I planned a surprise visit to Etah. Shalu was unable to hide her excitement when I reached late on Friday. She showed me a beautiful little house that she had made from the chocolate boxes which I had brought for her during my first visit. I was pleased with her creativity and the secret intention behind it that our home would be "Home Sweet Home". We all chatted till late night and then went to sleep.

The next morning, the news about my visit spread to the rest of the family members in Parmesh Sadan. Shalu's Bua – the Tingals, the only family not staying in Parmesh Sadan, were notified and invited to meet me in the evening. After lunch, Shalu, Sharad Ji, some of her younger cousins, and I went to see a film at the Krishna Theatre, which was barely fifty metres away. After the show, Shalu asked me:

"How was the movie?"

"It was worth Rupee one," I replied instantly to increase her curiosity.

"What do you mean, each ticket was Rupees four?" Shalu questioned.

"There were two cabaret dances, each worth 25 paise and your company was worth 50 paise." My reply was yet another trap. This summed up the fact that the movie had two dances for cheap entertainment to attract the public.

"How come my company was just worth 50 paise?" Shalu seemed upset.

"With the company of so many brothers and sisters, how could I take advantage of your company for more than 50 Paise." I closed the conversation with a naughty smile.

That evening, we had fun with the whole extended family. We had a little musical night, some gossip, an exchange of interests, some philosophical discussions, tea, coffee, snacks, dinner and sweets to top up. At lunchtime, I insisted that Shalu and her family stay with me after their shopping in New Delhi. Etah was a small district, and most people did their shopping in Agra or New Delhi, especially for such occasions.

Back in Ghaziabad, I kept thinking about the cohesiveness within Shalu's joint family. It was not easy to differentiate between real and cousin brothers and sisters. This was a completely different Etah than I had experienced during my high school. My family did not appreciate my visit to Etah, which was against the norm.

As our wedding day approached, our close relatives expressed discomfort about attending two weddings -one after the other. They argued that it would be too tiring and risky to travel to Etah immediately after my elder brother, Ajay Ji's wedding. My wedding was rescheduled from December to 11th March the next year. As my cousin sister's marriage was already fixed for 13th March in Lucknow, it was decided that the venue of my marriage be shifted from Etah to Lucknow. This was bad news for Shalu's parents. They had to bear financial losses and the inconvenience of organising everything in an unknown city.

While renegotiating arrangements with Shalu's parents about the marriage, my parents developed some reservations. Neither Shalu nor I were aware of these complications. Even now, we both try to piece together the puzzle. Maybe my father got paranoid with the comparison to my cousin sister Alka's marriage. He was sure that her father, Naresh uncle, would put up a big show. He had a much better job and was posted in Lucknow. His office staff and colleagues would do everything possible to gain favour and make the best use of this occasion by giving expensive gifts. His son-in-law was also an engineer, making matters worse.

Another reason could be that my parents never expressed their expectations earlier and left Shalu's parents to do their best as she was their only daughter. Their family was among the most renowned families in Etah, but we were unaware that Ravindra Kumar had only earned name and fame, and not money. The gap for the best show between the two families grew evident as the marriage day approached.

After my elder brother Ajay Ji's marriage, Shalu, her mother, and Sharad Ji visited me in Ghaziabad for an overnight stay. They had spent the whole day shopping in New Delhi. The next day, I tried to impress them with my cooking. Shalu was standing next to me in the kitchen as I was giving the finishing touch to the lentil in the *Kadai* on my 2-litre gas stove, which was not very stable with the Kadai on it. It was a bad move, and the Kadai toppled.

Shalu instinctively put out her hand to save me from the thick boiling lentils. In the process, she suffered a bad burn. I also had a small splash on my toe, but it was nothing compared to what Shalu had on her hand. I was upset with myself. Sharad Ji was almost crying. Shalu's mother tried to get some home medication to reduce the burning. Shalu was hiding her pain. She was concerned for me. Indian kitchens are full of risks, and we do little to make them safe. Now, it became a priority for me to get a proper gas connection and stove. Back at Etah, the exact details of the accident were not disclosed. Shalu proved that she would stand between me and my bad luck.

When I arrived at Lucknow for my marriage, I sensed that things were not right. My father expressed his annoyance very strongly and asked for my cooperation. This would have resulted in a last-minute marriage break-up unless all the conditions were met. Shalu had shown her courage by trying to save me from the accident in my kitchen. Now it was my turn to stand between her and my father and take up all the heat. I politely refused to cooperate.

My parents knew that I would not let this marriage fail even if I had to go alone for the wedding. No one in my family dared to go against my father. Generally, relatives add fuel to the fire. But in this case, the division was clear. On one side, I stood alone, all by myself. On the other side was the entire Johari family. I had to endure mental torture every day. My father's introduction of me to any new relative who arrived for the occasion was far from ideal. My greatest sin was that I had been seeing Shalu before the marriage ceremony, making the marriage merely a formality.

Marriages are very costly, and my father told me that he was running out of budget. I reminded him that I had wanted a simple wedding. However, as far as I was concerned, it was still not too late, and we could minimise further expenses by not engaging a Band for the Barat, the marriage procession, and for the reception later. At the time, I was unaware that no one was interested in solutions. For them, their problem was much more important than the solution, and it should remain unsolved.

A person's status in society is determined by the magnitude and quantity of the problems that they face rather than by the ability to find simple solutions to complex issues. At a gathering, people are not interested in capturing the best moments, instead, they take photos, raise their latest mobile phones to establish their supremacy.

My unexpected advice further fuelled my father's anger, but he agreed to my suggestion. He wanted to teach me a lesson on how impractical and unsocial my ideas were. His intentions were good, like bitter medicines. This would ensure that I was cured and would abstain from silly advices in future. However, the child within me never grew up. To date, I have failed to stop delivering my simple resolutions. Nevertheless, those around me have grown wiser and no longer reveal their complicated problems to me.

On the wedding day, everyone's spirits were quite low due to the absence of the Band. The motivation to get dressed in the best attire was absent. There was no hurry to reach the marriage venue, which was the Gomti Hotel. We took Ravindra Kumar and his relatives by surprise, by arriving silently at the marriage place. There was confusion for some time as to whether this was an attempt by the crowd to capture the party for a free dinner until Shalu's elder brothers identified some of us.

Amid this confusion, the marriage ceremonies were performed. The waiters could not get their tip money from me as they failed to identify who the bridegroom was. I had taken off my jacket and looked like any other ordinary-dressed member. When Shalu asked me what the matter was, I told her quietly that she should be thankful to God that we were there. She had no clue what was happening, and my answer went above her head.

As she reached our home the next day, things started getting clearer to her. My relatives were more interested in judging the clothes, jewellery, and other metals that Shalu had brought with her rather than in getting familiar with her. Everyone was convinced that Shalu's parents had done a lousy job and had taken advantage of my parents' simplicity. Shalu was in a state of utter shock and trembled inside with fear.

This was the first time in her life that she felt neglected. I did not wish to make things worse, so I remained silent. However, I consoled Shalu and urged her to trust me. I advised her against taking matters into her own hands and encouraged her not to respond to any queries, as this would only aggravate the situation. Shalu and I returned to Ghaziabad after attending my cousin sister Alka's wedding, which was scheduled just two days after our marriage.

14. GHAZIABAD

We were happy to return to our one-room set in Ghaziabad. It was roughly mid-day. This was the first time that we both had complete privacy. I locked the room, and was trying to be romantic. Shalu looked at me helplessly and told me in a low voice that she was suffering from a severe headache. She had not slept properly since the marriage. The house in Lucknow was small and crowded. Daytime had been even more confusing and scary for her. All this took a significant toll on her health. She was drained mentally and physically. I asked her to rest and joined her. This was the first time I took her in my arms. Her head rested on my shoulder. My hand was on her head, touching her very softly. I kissed her forehead to express my love and sympathy. I asked her to try to sleep. In less than a minute, she was fast asleep in my arms.

After about an hour, I slipped out of bed and went to the kitchen. I prepared food so that we could enjoy it later in peace. After finishing the kitchen work, I returned to the room. Shalu was still fast asleep. I turned on the TV at a very low volume. This was a small, Black & White, solid-state Uptron TV. It was from the lot that was imported and thus very cute. Being relatively light, moving or fitting it into a small corner space was easy.

The timing was perfect for one of my favourite series, *"The Sea World"*. I could submerge myself and watch it quietly. Had it been a popular cartoon such as Donald Duck or Pluto, other favourites of mine, I could not have controlled my simultaneous unrestricted laughter and crying. This would have disturbed her sleep. A soft voice brought me back from the sea world to the real world.

"What are you watching?" This was Shalu. She was looking refreshed.

"*The Sea World*, my favourite show. How are you feeling now? Would you like some tea?" I asked enthusiastically.

"Tea would be great. I will get it for you. Give me five minutes." Shalu showed her initiative.

"Don't worry, you take rest. You know that I can prepare tea." I smiled to remind her of my first cup of tea for her in this very room.

I left the room, leaving her to enjoy the TV show. As I returned with the tea and some snacks, Shalu seemed a bit confused. She asked me.

"What is there to watch in this programme? There are only some fishes and no humans. There is no story either." It was obvious that she had not seen any documentaries about the animal kingdom. I placed the tea and snacks on the table and moved it closer to the bed.

"These whales are truly magnificent creatures, standing proud as the largest animals in our oceans! Interestingly, they are not fish but mammals, just like us. They give birth to fully developed calves and nurture them with their milk. Just like us, they need to come to the surface to breathe. Did you know that the sea covers about two-thirds of our planet? That means our land is just one-third of the Earth's surface, making the ocean twice as vast! With so many diverse species, the underwater world is crowded with life! Sometimes, we forget that humans are not the only species on this planet. There is so much to discover about these amazing animals. These documentaries fill me with awe and curiosity about ocean life and its creatures." I could have gone on and on, but I saw that Shalu was not ready for yet another severe headache and looked at me for mercy.

"You can talk," Shalu smiled and picked up the tea.

"You didn't tell me how your headache is. Did you have a good nap?" I asked her while sipping tea and getting close to her.

"I am a lot better now. I slept like a child. It must have been about three hours at least. What did you do during this time?" Shalu was relaxed.

"The dinner is ready. There is plenty of time for dinner. If you like, we can go to the market. It is not far, and you will enjoy it." I proposed.

"That's a good idea. Give me about half an hour. I want to change." The offer was accepted.

A little later, we went downstairs to say hello to our landlord, Sharma Ji, and I introduced Shalu to him. Shalu looked gorgeous. She was dressed casually in blue jeans and a long top. Although she had celebrated her twentieth birthday only a couple of months earlier, she looked like a schoolgirl due to her thin structure. We knocked at the door, and Mrs Sharma opened the door.

"*Namaste,* Aunty Ji. How are you? This is Shalu. We came today after our marriage. I will be going to the office tomorrow. I thought I should introduce her to you if she needs any help during the day." By now, Mr Sharma and his two sons and a daughter had joined us and were looking curiously at Shalu but in a welcoming gesture.

"Oh, sure. Feel free to call us if you need anything. I am mostly at home and hardly go anywhere," Mrs Sharma replied.

We greeted everyone and departed.

"Sharma Ji and his family are very nice and helpful. Do not be shy; call them if you need any help," I reiterated. After walking only a few steps, we noticed someone calling us.

"Bhaiya Ji, have you got married? Where are you going? I will take you there." This was the young *Rikshaw* puller I had engaged several times, as I had no conveyance. His voice was full of joy. I could not turn down the offer.

"Yes, we just came today after our marriage. I want to show her the market," I answered as we both took our seats in his Rikshaw.

"I will drop you at *Ghanta Garh*. When you are done, just check at the same place, and I will take you back as well." The Rikshaw puller told us enthusiastically. For some people, happiness has nothing to do with money. He worked hard all day for so little money but he was always cheerful. I was about to bulldoze Shalu with my philosophy when she interrupted.

"Is he your friend?" Shalu asked in a very low tone. She was sceptical about my friend circle.

"He operates from the crossing next to our home. The people here are very friendly," I resisted with a smile.

In the next few days, the same incident repeated during our walk around the locality. The sugarcane juice hawker, the owner of the tea stall, and the milkman at the corner all had similar questions and offers. Every time this happened, Shalu looked at me with suspicion and fear. Her brother Sharad Ji had not done a good job by not investigating his friends. This boy is ridiculous. She was wondering if her Raj aunty's words would be proved correct.

Shalu fasted on Mondays. This day of the week is devoted to Lord Shiva who is known for leading a very unorthodox life-style among all the Gods. He applies ash from the burial ground on his body. His friends are not from a cultured society but are ghosts and the overlooked ones. Every now and then on a Monday, Raj aunty would caution her, "Stop fasting on Mondays, Shalini, or else you will get a husband like Lord Shiva." All these events would have shocked an ordinary person and compelled one to change course, but Shalu was not an ordinary girl. She was an exceptional girl. She continued fasting religiously every Monday.

At home, Shalu was busy upskilling her cooking during the daytime when I was away for work. She was not getting much success. She would taste the cooked food and throw it into the service lane. This continued for a few weeks, which attracted pigs who would devour it with great pleasure and invite their friends as well to enjoy the feast. One day, we overheard Mrs Sharma, our landlady, complaining to her husband that since Mr Johari has got married, she has noticed an increase in pigs in the service lane.

Once Shalu's cooking became edible, she started experimenting on me and my friends. She was excited about her new skills and the creative preparations and would offer me dinner soon after I returned from work. As this was the peak of my hunger, I overate every time. This made me lethargic and resulted in me sleeping early, which bored Shalu for the next two or three hours. A few days later, as this routine continued, she asked me:

"Do you love me?" Her voice was tinged with sadness. Her gaze was steady, fixed on mine as if searching for an answer that words might fail to convey—perhaps believing that love could be spoken more powerfully through the eyes than mere words.

"Why are you asking this? What happened?" I was not expecting this question.

"Do you love me? I want to know," Shalu repeated, holding tightly to her emotions.

"Do you feel ignored? Do you feel that I am not taking care of you? Do you feel I am making up things and not enjoying your company? Don't you feel honesty and transparency in my every word and behaviour? Don't you enjoy my company? Have I hurt you in any way?" As I showered her with questions, Shalu interrupted me.

"It is not that at all. I love you. I have loved you since we first met, but I am not sure about you." Shalu poured out her heartfelt feelings.

"I don't really know what love is. For me, love is not what is depicted in movies. I cannot love at first sight. I feel all this is just physical attraction. Maybe girls are much more emotional than boys, but I am not that emotional. I cannot pretend. Let me know if I ever ignore or hurt you. Give me some time, and I will tell you when I will be in love. I will love you more than anyone. I will love you beyond your imagination. But please give me some time." I hugged Shalu.

"I believe you, but tell me why do you go to sleep straight after dinner. Why are we not going out like we used to? I get bored. I cannot sleep so early," Shalu confessed.

"Oh! Is that it? Haven't you seen the dog downstairs? That is a stray dog, but our kind landlord offers it food every day. That is enough for the dog, and it sleeps there all day. The same goes for me. You give me dinner straight after work, and I have no choice but to sleep after the tasty and fulfilling dinner." I clarified.

"Okay, so from now on you won't be getting dinner straight after work. Then you will not complain," Shalu smiled.

I was pleased with her cooking and did not miss any chance of appreciating and encouraging her. Shalu developed a keen interest in cooking and surpassed everyone's expectations. As a rule, when you get tasty Indian food, you can be almost sure that it is full of fat and spices. However, her preparations had just a little touch of fat and spices. I don't remember any meal which I consumed without appreciating her cooking. It is always tasty and healthy. In Melbourne, Shalu is very popular among all my friends and their children for her cooking. The passion and love with which she prepares food for anyone is the crux of our friendships, despite my ugly sense of humour.

We were having a good time in our one-room set. As dinner was not served straight after work, we would go out in the evening to watch a movie, or go to a South Indian restaurant, or go to the nearby B Block market for *Panni Puri* and *Chaat*. This market had a restaurant that I used to visit for dinner as a bachelor when I was not in the mood to cook. It also had a small clinic which was on our company's panel, and which we could reach out for general medication and advice.

Shalu often ordered *Idli* in Udupi, while I would go for *Utapam* or *Dosa*. After much persuasion that Shalu could also order *Utapam* or *Dosa* instead of the cheapest item, *Idli*, she kept sticking to *Idli*. She always told me that it was not about money, but because it was her favourite dish. Finally, I gave up. Even today, her favourite dish in a South Indian restaurant is *Idli*.

I had a favourite Bakery shop in the main market, *Madhurima*, that we would never miss. Shalu also developed a taste for it. At home, Shalu was getting used to the strange phenomenon that I could laugh alone in a room. She would often come to check and find me watching Donald Duck or Pluto cartoons by Walt Disney. I would be laughing hysterically, with non-stop tears falling from my eyes. Sometimes, she whispered, "What a joke, I am married to a child".

One day, my elder brother, Abhay Ji, visited us. He had been selected for the Indian Forest Services (IFS) and had to report to Delhi for his medical and physical tests. This required him to complete a distance of 25-km in four hours, which was a tough call. He was a bit nervous but in great spirits. He had been preparing himself for this. He was also selected for IAS, but his rank was not the best, so he joined the IFS. I was delighted with his selection. After all, he had fulfilled our parents' dream. My father had many expectations from me, but I had disappointed him. At least someone in our family could raise the flag so high that it would take generations within our extended family to match this honour. He completed his medical and physical tests and returned to Lucknow the next day.

Approximately three months after our marriage, we received invitations to two weddings. My cousin brother, Manoj Kudesia, and Shalu's cousin brother, Sanjay Tingal, were getting married. The weddings were so close that it was impossible to attend both. We decided to attend Manoj Ji's wedding and then go back to Etah for the reception ceremony of Sanjay Dada. My parents, elder brother Ajay Ji, and his wife, Menu Bhabhi, visited Sahaswan, an outer suburb in Badaun, for Manoj Ji's wedding. This was their ancestor's house, where Manoj Ji's father and uncle lived with their families. This was my first visit to Sahaswan. As anticipated, Shalu and I found ourselves isolated, while my parents highly recommended Ajay Ji and Menu Bhabhi to all the relatives who attended the celebrations. Shalu was not in her best health, and I spent most of my time around her.

Back to Etah, we rested for the night. The following morning, we planned to visit the Tingal's home to congratulate Sanjay Dada and Ranjana Bhabhi, as this would not be possible during the reception ceremony in the evening. Shalu's younger cousin brothers had alerted them. We knew that the Tingal brothers would tease us into elaborating on all the enjoyable experiences that a newly married couple undergoes. As we reached their house, Jag uncle and Shail aunty were on the veranda with their two elder sons and the son-in-law Jayant Ji, an Army Officer. We had hardly finished greeting everyone when a somewhat vulgar remark by Jayant Ji blew my fuse. In response, I asked him, in a very firm tone, how he would feel if I used the exact wordings for his wife, Rani Didi. No one expected such a response, as Jayant Ji had a very high stature in age and relationship.

This was my first visit to their home after my marriage, and I made it very clear that now Shalu was not a little girl anymore who belonged to their family. She was now my wife. One must think twice before messing with her. I was not scared of the age or status of a person. We spent about an hour there and then returned to Parmesh Sadan. Though we joined the evening reception ceremony, I kept a flat face to communicate that I would not revisit them unless some drastic measures were taken. Shalu was a bit sad about the chain of events as Rani Didi was her best friend, but she could also appreciate my stand.

After returning to Ghaziabad, we found that Shalu was pregnant. My parents believed that my first child would come much earlier, knowing the secret of our premarital relationship. We disappointed them by telling them that we were expecting our child around our first marriage anniversary. My parents asked us to look for at least a two-room flat so they could stay with us to help during the delivery. My friend, the milkman, helped us in finding a two-room set nearby. Due to his good references, we had no difficulty in finalising the deal. We could still use the services of the same young Rikshaw puller, who had been tagged as my friend by Shalu.

One day, some of my junior colleagues who had graduated from BHUIT and had joined BE Ghaziabad, came to watch the movie "King Kong" with us. For Shalu, this was her first experience of such a film, and it was an eye-opener. Almost every day she was discovering a new world with me. How could they create such a realistic character and story? Shalu admired the technology used in Hollywood movies. When the movie finished, Shalu could not stand due to severe pain in both her legs. She was so thin that her body was probably not prepared to bear a child. My friends were in a fix.

I looked at Shalu, who was still struggling to get up. I lifted her in my arms and walked out of the theatre. My friends surrounded me like bodyguards. People around me thought that King Kong had inspired me so much that I was pretending to be like him. As we came out, a Rikshaw puller rushed towards us like an ambulance. This was the same young Rikshaw puller who had dropped us here earlier and was back in time for us. He was concerned for Shalu's health and suggested a nearby clinic. I requested him to take us home.

In a couple of days when Shalu got a little better, I took her to a nearby Gynaecologist, Dr Ila Amba, who was on my company's panel of specialist doctors. After a brief wait, it was our turn. Once we greeted her, I recounted my version of the story. I asked for her assistance, emphasising that this was my first experience. I was uncertain about the entire process and whether we could afford a baby, given Shalu's health. The doctor looked at me as if she was a psychiatrist and I was the patient needing emergency treatment.

"Mr Johari, I understand that this is probably a first experience for her as well. If you don't mind, please stay outside and let me complete her medical examination." In one small sentence, Dr Illa had set me right. I was impressed by her intelligence and sense of humour, and I felt sympathy for the people who had been a target of my similar crude humour. We visited her regularly, but I ensured that I always stayed outside, except when Dr Illa called me into the cabin after the medical examination to discuss some issues relating to the medical officer in my company.

Though we were settling well into our new two-room set, we missed our first house, which symbolised our first love. We still miss it and never miss an opportunity to recall or narrate our first meeting. Shalu became friendly with the lady of the family who rented the front portion of this two-storey house. The landlord's family lived on the upper level.

Mr Gopal Verma, a manager at my company who was about twelve years my senior, lived only three blocks away at the T-intersection. Who would have thought that Verma Ji and his family would also migrate to Melbourne soon after we did in 1995 and become our family friends? My cousin brother, Manoj Kudesia had also shifted into the two-room set in our next house. His wife's name was also Shalini, and we used to call her Bhabhi Ji as a sign of respect. Just three months after her marriage, she also got pregnant. I had already nick-named both the babies, Dharminder as my baby and Parminder as Manoj Ji's baby, as if I was sure both babies were boys.

One day, we got the good news that the marriage of Shalu's eldest brother, Raju Dada (Pradeep Ji), was settled. Incidentally, the name of his fiancée was also Shalini, but as the name of the sister and wife cannot be the same, Shalu's family called her Pinky. Shalu's parents wanted to honour us with the privilege of stamping this relationship and brought her to our place to meet and greet. Shalu was extremely excited to welcome her and had decided to cook Samosas at home. They didn't turn out well, so we repurposed them into bread rolls at the last moment. Even though I was not particularly impressed by Pinky Ji, our approval was merely a formality, and I refrained from vetoing.

Around halfway through Shalu's pregnancy, my parents came to visit us. We had no prior information. It was a hot and humid afternoon. I was at work, and Shalu was fast asleep. They must have knocked on the door for at least fifteen minutes, when the lady from the front house came to help them. Our portion had a sliding door built of iron grill, which allowed us to see through when it was closed. Finally, when Shalu opened the door, she saw my parents and rushed back to get dressed in a Sari.

Traditionally, a daughter-in-law wears a sari instead of trousers and top like an unmarried girl. Tired and thirsty, my parents had to wait outside for another ten minutes, which made them furious. Poor Shalu had to cope with it. No excuse was accepted. My parents stayed for about a week, and Shalu looked after them well. It was strange to see her in a sari all the time, especially in the hot and humid weather.

When it was close to Shalu's delivery, my parents came to help. Shalu's mother also joined us. I took Shalu to Dr Illa's clinic one evening as she had started her contractions. She stayed there for about two hours, but it was a false call, and we were sent back. Later that week, we revisited Dr Illa as she planned to go overseas for two weeks. After a quick checkup, Shalu was taken to the labour room. We had a son just before midnight through the natural process. Dr Illa gave me the good news. I asked her about Shalu. I could not enjoy the moment until I was convinced that she was doing well.

"Have you thought about your son's name? There is no hurry. Let me know by morning. I need to put it on the Birth Certificate," Dr. Illa said.

"Manu, Manu Johari," I replied. Shalu and I had had many discussions about this and had come up with the name Abhimanyu. This is a character in the mythological *Mahabharat*. However, this was not approved by our parents, as Abhimanyu was killed at a young age in the Great War. As a result, we cut this name short and adopted Manu, the name in reserve, as his nickname. Another reason for choosing Manu was that he was the first in our family. Although I was the youngest in my family, Manu would be the eldest in the next generation.

"You can see your wife and son. If everything goes well, you can take her home tomorrow evening," Dr Illa instructed.

I was pleased to see Shalu and Manu. Shalu appeared very tired yet happy. Manu was asleep. I examined him closely for any signs of hair on his head but failed to notice any trace of hair on his face as well, which included his eyebrows and eyelids. The top of his head was very soft as it moved up and down with his breathing. I murmured, "I am sure that Dr Illa has counted his fingers and toes to ensure that he is not lacking anything other than hair." I kissed Shalu on her forehead and told her to rest and that I would join her in the morning.

The news delighted my parents and Shalu's mother, particularly because it was a son. When Shalu's father heard the news over the phone the following morning, he informed us that he had already known about it and told us the exact time the baby boy was born:

"I was sleeping last night when I dreamed that a saint-like person in white clothes was standing before me. The saint said I am coming to see you and turned into a baby boy lying beside me. I got up from sleep and checked the time. It matches with the time you have told us. Shalu has been gifted with a great soul." Shalu's father was excited to tell us about his dream.

A few days later, he joined us for the ceremony that is traditionally held on the tenth day of a baby's birth. My parents and brothers were also there for this occasion, accompanied by Shalu's parents and brothers. We still wonder how, in those days, we could fit ten to fifteen people in such a small house. Nowadays, everyone requires their own room, still one craves for additional space. Shalu's parents and brothers returned to Parmesh Sadan after a couple of days. My parents stayed with us for a few more days and then returned to Lucknow with my elder brothers and Menu Bhabhi.

My eldest brother, Dada, decided to stay with us for some more days. This was the first time that Dada stayed with us all by himself. Due to our age difference, I had never had the chance to understand him. I had lots of questions for him. What was his opinion about all his younger brothers and sister? What did he remember about our grandparents and uncles? Most of my memories of Dada were after he had gone into depression. One thing I was sure of was that his misfortune was not just for him; it had also changed our family's destiny. I did not have much time to spend with him in the mornings as I had to catch the company bus around 7:30 am.

During the day, Dada spent most of his time with Manu. He did not fuss about meals. He encouraged Shalu to wear comfortable dresses instead of a sari all the time. He was happy to walk around and shop for vegetables from nearby shops, as the hawkers did not always bring the best. In the evening, we all went for walks or to the nearby market to enjoy fast food. This was the best time to chat and get to know him.

"You know, when we got the record player for the first time, you bought three vinyls. They were amazing, and I found two of them in the cassette. These days, hardly anyone buys vinyl. They are expensive and delicate, though the sound quality is unmatchable." I was lost in the time when the first vinyl played, and the whole room was filled with music. The songs were the best collections by music director Madan Mohan. Dada had bought a famous ABBA collection. I had no knowledge of English music, but those songs infatuated me.

"Who was that doctor? You had taken me a few times when I was a kid and had run high fever." I was getting nostalgic.

"Zero Narayan, he is doing very good now. He still practices at the same place. His actual name was Awadesh Narayan, but he spelt it strangely, starting with 'O' instead of 'A'- O W A D E S H - so I started calling him Zero Narayan." Dada laughed. He had an innocent smile. He looked like a 35-year-old child. He had a pure heart. He never held a grudge against anyone. Since he went into depression, everyone started correcting him. Everyone would point out to him. "Why are you doing this? Why are you standing here? Why are you looking at me like this?" Every one of us, all his younger brothers and sister, started treating him like a younger sibling. By no standards were we respectful to him.

I always sympathise with my parents as they had to deal with all the hard times, and I could discount them somewhat, but all of us were equally guilty. Since moving to BHU, I had developed a soft corner for Dada and always paid him due respect. After getting married, I could not even dream of disrespecting him. Shalu had never mistreated anyone, so her new relationship with Dada was flawless, pure, enjoyable, respectful, and friendly.

"Atul told me about a cartoon column in the Hindi Newspaper *Swatantra Bharat* that you were very fond of. What was that?" Shalu asked.

"He must be talking about Aj Ji. In Sanskrit, Aj means goat. In this cartoon, a man with a goat head would mock one of the main news stories. They must have derived Aj from Aaj, meaning today. Something special about today. I always found it amusing as Aj Ji is so close to Ajay Ji." Dada could not stop laughing. Ajay Ji was my elder brother but younger to Dada.

"Do you still need to take the medicines?" I asked curiously.

"These days, I am on just a maintenance dose. I am getting good sleep and feel relaxed during the day. To some extent, I can adjust the dose myself." Dada explained in a normal tone.

"Are you in touch with some of your college or university friends?" I continued the conversation.

"Not really. I never had many friends. You know Sachdeva was my classmate. Now, he runs the busiest pharmacy shop near IT Crossing." Dada had a smile on his face.

"What happened to your married life?" I asked. I was curious, as they had hardly lived together. I gathered all my courage to ask about this sensitive issue. Hopefully, this would not spoil his mood. He looked in high spirits.

"She was never interested in marriage. I do not know why she agreed to get married. I only stayed for a few days at her railway quarter and then returned home. She was staying with her mother and a brother. She was happy there and did not want to move to our place. If she did that, she would have had to surrender her allocated residence, and her mother and brother would have nowhere to go. We did not develop any physical or emotional relationship, so it did not bother me." Dada was not upset. I was amazed at his attitude.

How boldly and naturally he had moulded himself to another inhuman verdict of life. We had reached the Udupi restaurant, and the boy came to take our order.

"I will have *Uttapam*. What would you like, Dada?" I requested.

"Can I order a *Masala Dosa*." Dada asked.

"I will go for *Idli Sambhar*." Shalu completed her order.

"Why did you choose *Idli*? Why not *Dosa* or *Uttapam*?" Dada was curious. Shalu looked at me and smiled.

"You both think alike," Shalu said softly and kept smiling. Dada looked at me, somewhat confused.

"Nothing, even I don't understand it." I closed the conversation.

Dada stayed with us for another month and then returned to Lucknow. We have very vivid memories of his stay. We enjoyed his company. During his stay with us, he was perfectly normal. We felt as if he had never been a patient of depression. After Dada returned, Shalu went to Etah to live with her parents for about a month to rest and recover.

15. SAHIBABAD

I was enjoying my time at BE Ghaziabad. About seven of the fifteen batchmates who had joined BE in 1984 had moved on to other companies or countries. I was also under pressure to cope with inflation, as the rates were increasing rapidly while salaries were not keeping pace. My friends Kamarjit Singh, who worked with me in the NC Programming Cell, and Anil Nijhawan, who worked in the Production Control Department, were contemplating starting a venture. Anil, from the same batch, was an alumnus of IIT Delhi. We also participated in a kitty party that was hosted by Kamarjit's father for some financial benefit. Following Kamarjit's suggestion, Anil and I formed a trio to enter the kitty as a single unit. Each of us would share the money equally and benefit together.

This decision brought the three of us closer, and we were now working very seriously on starting a computer training program for schools. I decided to move closer to work to coordinate better. This was a difficult and expensive decision. The rent was reasonably high in this locality and I required my conveyance as the company bus would not pick me up from such a close distance. Any popular scooter brand had a long booking queue. People took advantage of this by making multiple bookings and then selling at higher rates to the needy.

Since I could not afford additional money, I resorted to the Girnar Scooter instead of the more popular and reliable Bajaj Scooter. I was happy with it because it looked the same as the Bajaj Scooter. At the time, I had no concept of brand image and did not know how much effort and quality control were required to build a brand image. Now, I believe that we must work tirelessly to develop our brand so we can be proud of our name. Today, I proudly introduce myself at any party or to a new friend as:

"I am Shalini's husband."

I do not need any more explanation. People nod their heads in affirmation. Yes, they know who I am talking about. Shalu is everyone's best friend, especially all the ladies in our friend circles. She has all the time in the world to listen to them patiently, not just once but several times, about their worries, their grievances, and anything and everything that life has given them or has mistreated them.

Shalu has complete sympathy with everyone and genuinely feels their pain. They are sure that their secrets are safe with her and will not be leaked. If they come in person to unload their mental pressure, they also get the best tea and freshly cooked tasty and healthy snacks. They also find a unique collection of kitchen items, dresses, accessories, and household items. They know that Shalu will not only guide them in the right direction but will also hold their hands, take them to the respective shops, and, if possible, help them get a better bargain. They know that they can ask for any plant that looks healthy and happy in Shalu's sunroom and return it to her in a week if it does not like the environment of the new place. They know that their kids and husbands will be happy and cheerful to visit her house in person or in a group during a party. They also envy Shalini as she always stands out in a crowd despite her simple dresses and no apparent makeup.

This reminds me of the punch line in the 1980s advertisement of Onida TV:

"Neighbour's envy. Owner's pride."

I believe that Shalu and I are like the main characters in Walt Disney's animated movie *'Beauty and the Beast'*, with the difference being that the Beast lost its animal behaviour and turned into a handsome prince with just one kiss from the Beauty. However, even after hundred kisses, the animal within me has not melted away, and all my friends maintain a safe distance from me.

Coming back, we shifted to a house about 50 metres from the BE Executive Colony in Chandra Nagar. The Industrial area around this locality, Sahibabad, was just about a kilometre away from my office. The closest locality, which was part of New Delhi, Vivek Vihar, was about two kilometres away. We had barely settled in this new residence when my elder brother Abhay Ji and his batchmate Ranjana Ji visited us one day. Both were undergoing administrative training in New Delhi after their selection in IFS. It was evening, and we were having a good time and chatting about different things when we were interrupted by a knock on our gate. It was a special postal delivery, Telegram, used for urgent messages.

"Dada is no more. Come Soon - Prem." The postman delivered the message and asked us to sign to confirm its delivery.

We were shocked. Abhay Ji started crying. Ranjana Ji tried to console him. Our neighbours helped us in getting a taxi to Lucknow. Shalu did all the packing. On our way to Lucknow, we dropped Ranjana Ji at her residence in Ghaziabad. We halted at Etah, in Parmesh Sadan, almost halfway between Ghaziabad and Lucknow. This provided Manu with a much-needed break so we could change his clothes and get some fresh, hot milk. Shalu's father and elder brother, Sharad Ji, joined us for the remaining journey to Lucknow. We reached Lucknow early in the morning. As we knocked on the outer steel gate, my mother came and unlocked the gate. She was agitated and looked at Shalu, who was just ahead of us. Shalu tried to touch her feet as part of greetings and respect.

"What have you done to Dada in one month? He committed suicide soon after returning from Ghaziabad." She was so furious that she could have hit her. I pulled Shalu back and held my mother to console her.

"Let us all go inside. You can tell us in detail what happened." I could see that she was devastated at the loss of her eldest son, just at the age of thirty-five. She was confused and searching for a reason to console herself. My father had also come out and looked perplexed and angry. He was not expecting Ravindra Kumar and Sharad Ji. As we entered the lounge and settled a bit, I asked.

"How did this happen? Dada was fine just a few months ago."

"He fell into depression soon after returning to Lucknow. He kept worrying about our financial burden now that I am retired. He was extremely anxious about the cost of medicines and treatment. He was concerned about Ajay Ji's work, which was not improving. He poisoned himself." Papa Ji explained.

I had no additional questions. My mind replayed the words of my youngest uncle, a doctor, who had come to our wedding in Lucknow and had advised my father about Dada's condition. At that time, Dada had become somewhat agitated due to the overall atmosphere.

"*Bhai Sahab*, you should not worry much about Arun's aggressive behaviour. The real issue for such patients is when they are in deep depression. Then they cannot think of anything apart from ending their life."

His words had materialised. We were mistaken in thinking that Dada had almost recovered from his mental condition because of the wonderful time that we had recently shared with him. The cremation had already taken place as it was not possible to preserve the body after the postmortem. No police case was registered due to his medical history. Shalu's father and brother departed to stay with their relatives, Umesh Mama. We remained in Lucknow for a few days.

A month later, my parents came to visit us. This was a positive decision to help them cope with the grief of losing their eldest son, Dada. My mother took excellent care of Manu, giving him full body oil massages two to three times daily. She also brought a special pillow to maintain the shape of his head and would gently massage the softer part of his head with oil, helping it to become firmer. My father was constantly watchful to ensure that I did not mishandle Manu.

Manu received abundant affection from both his grandparents. He was the eldest and so far, the only grandchild. My parents also felt somewhat closer to us and were attempting to overlook our mistakes. When I told my mother about the Kitty and my plans to set up a computer coaching business, she did not like it. In her opinion, the Kitty concept was risky and beyond her comprehension. She also advised me to concentrate on my job, which offered a steady income and to manage my expenses more effectively. She was efficient and good at financial management.

My father seemed happy and relaxed. Manu kept us busy with doctors. The more care we took, the more frequently he fell sick. He was not eating well, and his iron level was dropping. Just before his first birthday, he was given a blood transfusion that I donated. Our blood group and other parameters had matched. After the blood transfusion, his complexion became darker, and for about two to three days, he remained like a drunk person, which was most apparent in his walk.

His diet improved for some time. The change in the complexion got so deep-seated in my mind that whenever Shalu's complexion got extra fair, I would take her to the doctor and complain about her complexion and request a blood test to check her Ferritin levels. Every time, my doubt was proved right, and she had to be given iron infusions three times over ten years.

Manu would also catch high fever and was prone to convulsions. When other options failed, we would give him a ride on the scooter to avoid the convulsions. The consistent fresh blow of air for about five to ten minutes would do the trick. This involved Manu catching a cold, but as per the doctor's advice, it was a much lower risk.

Once, Manu started breathing rapidly with wheezing. As it continued for two days, he was hospitalised. He was under the observation of his regular paediatrician, Dr Khanna, who was avoiding harsh treatment due to its side effects. It was about midnight on the fifth day when Shalu and I noticed that Manu was turning blue, and his breathing was becoming inconsistent. We panicked and contacted the young doctor who was on night duty. As per the norm, he could not change the medication. He contacted Dr Khanna, who rushed to the hospital. Manu was given steroids through intravenous injections. We kept praying. After a very long fifteen minutes, Manu coughed, and some mucus came out of his mouth.

As per the doctors, this was a good sign as it meant that Manu was responding to the treatment. Dr Khanna told us that Manu was having congestive heart failure, and thus he had to resort to this treatment, which he had been avoiding. Manu improved over the next four days. We brought him lots of balloons and toys and decorated his room. When Dr Khanna visited that night, he was pleasantly surprised and assured us that Manu could be discharged the following day.

For a few years, Manu remained on regular medication for Bronchitis. Much later, Dr Khanna expressed his concern when we told him about our migration to Melbourne. He told us that Melbourne was the world's capital regarding allergies, but Manu proved him wrong. We landed in Melbourne on 4th March 1995, on his eighth birthday. The first house we rented was on Manoon Road in Clayton. The house number was 31, representing 4 which as per numerology, is a lucky number for Manu. He has grown up to be an independent, handsome, fun-loving, intelligent, six-foot-plus young man. He joined the Australian Army at the tender age of eighteen. He worked hard to build his body and took initiatives to go on difficult deployments. We are proud of him.

Soon after my parents returned to Lucknow, Anil Nijhawan brought the good news that he had secured an order to deliver a crash course in computer education for a primary school in Kanpur. This was a one-week course which had to be completed before the end of September. There was much ground to cover. We had to buy a computer, prepare course materials, and tie up all the loose ends. Kamarjit and I worked through most of the tasks during office hours as we had access to a computer in our NC Programming Cell. We were excited but not prepared to leave our jobs yet. We finalised the date and booked tickets for all three of us.

Just then, I got the news that my elder brother Abhay Ji had decided to marry Ranjana Ji. The date of the marriage clashed with our coaching programme at Kanpur. The marriage ceremony was to be held at Ghaziabad from Ranjana Ji's residence. Obviously, I had to miss the marriage. Shalu was scared to live alone for a week. My friend, Pandya from BHUIT, who was two-years junior to me and was working in BE, agreed to stay in our house.

On the wedding day, my family reached Ranjana Ji's house from Lucknow. Shalu's family was also invited to the wedding. Shalu's father and Sharad Ji arrived to pick up Shalu and Manu on their way to the wedding. The wedding ceremony was in the afternoon. Shalu was prepared to attend the reception ceremony in Lucknow. However, my parents considered it a bad idea and sent them back.

Anil, Kamarjit, and I were pleased with our performance on our first contract, but we never secured a repeat order or any new business. We all learned that a successful business relies more on marketing than on the product itself. Soon, we had more bad news. The Kitty that we were a part of had to be abandoned. We would also not get our money back.

To recover his loss from the busted Kitty, Anil kept the computer and other equipment which we had purchased in the name of our business. These events soured our relationship. I learned a second life lesson: business should not be done with friends. I lost a lot in this process. I was paying higher rent by moving to Chandra Nagar. Kamarjit's dad compensated him, but I had to bear all the losses and the ongoing high rent.

During this time, we came to Parmesh Sadan to attend Raju Dada's marriage, Shalu's eldest brother. Just four days later, Shalu's cousin brother Babbi Dada was also getting married. I was reluctant to attend Babbi Dada's wedding due to the previous year's incident at Sanjay Dada's reception. This had strained our relations. We planned to return after attending Raju Dada's wedding. No one from the Tingal family was willing to risk disturbing the beehive by attempting to persuade me. All the relatives, including the Tingals, had come to attend Raju Dada's wedding. Everyone was getting ready to board the bus to depart to the bride's home. I had already taken a seat in one of the front rows. As Rani Didi entered the bus, we made natural eye contact. She paused momentarily at the door, then greeted me.

"Namaste, Atul Ji, how are you?"

"Namaste, Rani Didi. I am fine. How are you?" I replied equally respectfully.

"If you don't mind, would you attend Babbi's wedding?" She asked hesitantly.

"Why not?" I responded in a normal tone.

"Wow! That is great. We would love you to join us for Babbi's marriage. I will tell everyone now and invite you properly. I will be back in a minute." She exclaimed with joy and rushed back to Parmesh Sadan. Within no time, Rani Didi returned with her parents to formally invite us. Everyone was happy with this welcome news, but Shalu was most pleased. Shalu and Rani Didi hugged each other and kept smiling for a long time, crackling in disbelief from time to time.

Two days after returning from Babbi Dada's wedding, we were invited for lunch. All of us were sitting on their veranda, chatting and enjoying light snacks. After a while, I went inside to meet and greet Vinita Bhabhi, the new bride. I met her and Ranjana Bhabhi, wife of Sanjay Dada, in the kitchen. I was shocked to see old-style fireplace in the kitchen. How could an advanced family like this still stick to this cooking style and not switch to a gas stove? In my opinion, this was nothing short of torture and was inhumane for the ladies. I could not spend much time near the kitchen due to the smoke and guilt. When I came back to the veranda, I delivered my verdict.

"Sorry, Bua Ji and Phupha Ji, I am really upset to see the pain that both the Bhabhi's are taking to cook food for me. How come your kitchen still has such an old-style fireplace instead of a modern gas stove? I cannot believe it. I will have a meal today, but not again until you get a gas stove in the kitchen." Everyone noticed that I had lost all the charm of the meal and felt dejected. My eyes were fixed far in the sky. I had insulated myself from any excuse. This time, I had no intention of being rude. I was sad, lost, and confused. Nobody gave me any reason or tried to distract me. Back at Parmesh Sadan, Shalu was once again embarrassed and described a cut-down version of the episode. The very next day, we returned to Ghaziabad.

16. TOOL ROOM

Kamarjit and I were about to complete four years in the job and were due for promotion to Senior Engineer from Deputy Engineer. A few months before our promotion, we were transferred to different sections. I became in charge of the Tool Room which was located at the back of the Machining Hangar. It was not part of production and reported to the Tool Design department. While the Machine shop had a productivity index which they had to meet every month, the Tool Room did not have such a constraint as it was hard to estimate the time for fabricating any tool, jig, or fixture. This was mostly a skill-based job and required the ingenuity of the operators and supervisors.

Before I took over this section, it was headed by a senior manager, who had treated it as a below-dignity job. As a result, this area was in a mess, and employees had low morale. Two of the three supervisors were long overdue for promotion to the executive cadre. Kulshrestha Ji had only one more attempt left, while Arya Ji had two. The Tool Room Engineer shared Arya Ji's secret before joining section where he was transferred.

"Arya Ji comes from far and only works general shifts. You can assign him to the morning shift if he disobeys, and he will comply." Said the Engineer.

"What about Kulshrestha Ji?" I showed my curiosity.

"Oh, he is truly a gone case. It is impossible to motivate him to work. He aspires to be an executive, yet he is unwilling to put in any effort." The Engineer replied.

After the Engineer left the Tool Room to join his new department, I was the only executive in my section. I was very keen to get things moving and clear the backlog but did not get much support from the team. One day, I spoke to a machine operator:

"I am struggling to grasp the work style here. I can respect someone who works diligently like a horse and completes their tasks swiftly or outright refuses to work like a donkey. However, this in-between approach perplexes me, where one begins a task and then abandons it indefinitely."

The operator did not reply, but he took it to heart. He took the matter to the labour union and filed a complaint that I had called him a donkey. The matter reached the Deputy General Manager, who had joined recently from the Air Force. He was unfamiliar with the public sector culture or handling such a situation. He consulted his senior manager, who said that this lacked importance and was just a strength of test between the new section head and the staff. It would resolve itself; if not, they would handle it.

I was upset about this twist and how things had been taken out of context. I called my supervisors and explained the entire incident. I agreed with the operator that I had made a mistake, but this was my only error in two weeks. From here on, I would observe everyone from my cabin and note every mistake that anyone made. For the next two days I stayed in my cabin for the whole shift. This put all the operators and supervisors under tremendous pressure. They could not take the liberties that they had been taking for granted.

They had to be on the machine all the time. They could not afford to be away for even more than five minutes for any natural break as well. They could not gossip with each other. The stress was becoming unbearable for them. On the third day, just before the morning tea break, I approached the same operator, greeted him politely, and asked about his welfare. He was not expecting this and thought that I would grill him for all his mistakes in the last two days. He kept looking at me silently. I broke the silence.

"Meghraj Ji, I did not mean to insult you, and I'm sorry for hurting you. I recognize my mistake and appreciate that you all are more mature and wiser than I am. It seems my one mistake was taken quite seriously! I wanted to point out how many little mistakes we make daily. I promise I have no ill intentions, and I'm not keeping track of anything. I want everyone to feel relaxed and enjoy life like before, without unnecessary stress."

I spoke to the operator in a friendly tone and left the section for tea break. When I returned after half an hour, I saw that things looked normal. Operators were casually chatting again in groups of two or three. Everyone looked relaxed. By the next day, they had withdrawn their complaint. The matter had been resolved for everyone except me. I was still trying to get the hang of the issue. What had caused such a simple sentence to escalate into a major issue?

Very soon, I had an opportunity to attend a three-day training course on interpersonal relationships and behaviour. This was delivered in-house by an organisation formed by retired senior executives from various public sector undertakings. They had spent much of their professional career in HR departments and had dealt with industrial relations. Surprisingly, I found this training interesting and asked a lot of questions. I even discussed my recent encounter with my workforce.

The next morning, they conducted an exercise. It had two sets of questions; one was about our expectations from our managers, and the other was about our expectations from our workforce. I finished the questionnaires in no time. The trainer called me to the front to read my answers and took notes on the board. He then analysed my answers and declared that I am a dual personality. The way I expect my manager to behave with me, I behave opposite to that with my workforce. It was like I was in front of a mirror. Now, I expected the trainer to close the loop and provide answers to my fundamental problem.

"Mr Johari, when you approach an operator standing in front of the machine, you must first make an honest effort to understand his frame of mind. Is everything okay with him? Is he or any of his family members going through a tough time? What is bothering him? Do not just deliver your judgement through your body language or speech that he wastes time. To be respected, you must first learn to respect." The trainer simplified the concept for me.

After the training was over, I struggled to digest the concept. I had to shift myself from the centre of the universe. The annual appraisal for the entire workforce was due that week. My predecessor had left this job for me. Generally, in their previous assessments, Kulshrestha Ji and Arya Ji received scores between 4 and 6 out of 10 across various skills. I broke this trend and gave 96 out of 100 to Kulshrestha Ji and 94 to Arya Ji. As this was a confidential report, I handed it to the HR department in person. Within an hour,

Kulshrestha Ji and Arya Ji stood in my cabin.

"What have you done, Sir?" Asked Kulshrestha Ji. Though his eyes were wet, he was trying to control his expression of joy.

"What are you talking about? Please have a seat." I asked in a confused tone.

"Our appraisal that you have just submitted." Replied Kulshrestha Ji. Both had taken a seat and pulled it closer to my desk as if they were about to share a secret.

"But these are confidential reports, and I handed them over personally." I expressed my concern.

"We have been working in this organisation for over thirty years and have built our contacts. Why have you done this? We have not done anything great for you yet." They both looked thankful but confused.

"You do not have to prove anything to me. I'm sure that you must have put your heart, soul, and sweat into this organisation when you were young. If I ask you to show the same energy at this age, it will not be fair on my behalf. I must be mindful of the contributions made by both of you." I paused for a moment and then continued.

"Sorry, Arya Ji, I could not score you equal to Kulshrestha Ji. He has just one attempt left and needs two good appraisals to be considered for promotion to the executive cadre. There is still room for improvement in his next year's report. You have two more appraisals. I will bring it to the same level by then. This year, I will recommend only Kulshrestha Ji for promotion, but I promise you, Arya Ji, I will try my best for you next year." I provided my explanation for doing partiality and my intention of doing so.

"But what about Balram? Everyone likes him, and he has excellent ratings throughout." Arya Ji queried about the third supervisor, who was much younger than them.

"Oh, Balram is going to complete his degree very soon. He does not need this path. He can appear in competitions and get an executive position. He will have a much better career path that way. I have already suggested this to him. I think he understands." I clarified.

"Thank you, sir." This was the combined response from both of them. They stood with their palms joined in the posture of *Namaste* to express their gratitude. I stood up from my chair and shook hands with them. I could feel the warmth and zeal of both Kulshrestha Ji and Arya Ji. They left the cabin, but I could still see their expressions of disbelief. Even today, whenever I recall this incident, I still feel the same joy in my heart and energy in my palms.

Tool Room transformed with the energy and initiatives of Kulshrestha Ji and Arya Ji. I got continuous feedback and suggestions for improvement. All the operators were in high spirits. The backlog of the work was clearing fast. Small triangular metal pieces were installed high on places where pigeons visited so, they could not rest there and soil the floor and the raw materials stored below with their droppings. The tools and the raw materials were labelled and stacked nicely. Senior managers did not return halfway to the machine shop during routine visits. They were also proud to have a sneak peek of the Tool Room.

Vishwakarma day was approaching fast. *Vishwakarma* is the Engineer God, and this day is treated as an open day for the factory. I organised a party at my house for the Tool Room employees and everyone enjoyed a lot.

I had completed five years in BE. All our batch mates were promoted to the next level as senior engineers. A few months later, it was time for promotions for those who would jump from non-executive to executive cadre. I had already submitted another yearly appraisal for my supervisors. This was Kulshrestha Ji's last chance. He was nervous and busy going through technical books to prepare for the interview.

"What are you reading, Kulshrestha Ji? You look worried." I asked.

"Sir, I am preparing for the interview. This book is on production technology. They can be very technical in the interview." Replied Kulshrestha Ji.

"You cannot be sure about technical questions however hard you prepare. There will always be questions that you or I cannot answer. There is no point in wasting time. This will only make you nervous and spoil your interview. Just be normal and take it easy. Be who you are, and you will do your best. I will reach out to Mr Mathur later today to recommend your name," I assured Kulshrestha Ji.

Mr Mathur was the head of our division, and his recommendations were final. Later in the afternoon, I knocked on his office door.

"Who is there?" Mr Mathur asked.

"Sir, it is me. Johari." I responded.

"Come in." I slowly opened the door. As I looked inside, I felt embarrassed. Five managers were sitting before him, seemingly having an important meeting.

"Sorry Sir, I have disturbed your meeting. I will come later." I was apologetic.

"Tell me why you have come." Mr Mathur queried.

"Sir, tomorrow is the interview for the promotion to Assistant Engineer. I want to recommend Kulshrestha Ji from my section. This is his final attempt. Can you please consider him for the promotion? He has done an excellent job." I hurriedly said in a polite tone while standing close to the door.

"What about Mr Arya and Mr Balram? Don't you want to recommend them as well?" Asked Mr Mathur. All the managers were staring at me.

"Mr Arya has one more attempt left. I will leave him for next year. Mr Balram is completing his degree. He has a much brighter career ahead of him. Even otherwise, he is quite young." I provided the clarification and posted my recommendation for next year as well.

"You can go now." Mr Mathur had no further questions. I closed the door and returned to my desk. Later that afternoon, the machine shop manager, Mr Bhargav approached me.

"Johari, your man is going to be promoted. Congratulations." His tone had a tinge of envy.

"Why do you say so, Sir? I have not heard anything from Mr Mathur." I responded.

"After you were gone, Mr Mathur admonished us. He said we must learn from Johari, who recommended only one candidate for promotion with the best appraisals for two years. He has already chosen the candidate for next year as well. You all have recommended people from your section but have not given them good appraisals. What can I do if you have not done your part? Johari made my job simple." Mr Bhargav paused for a moment and shook my hand. "I am sure Mr Mathur will get your man promoted."

I was relaxed but knew that it was not solely on Mr Mathur and anything could happen. I abstained from sharing anything with Kulshrestha Ji. The interview went well for Kulshrestha Ji, but he was still stressed. Within the same week, the results were out, and Kulshrestha Ji had been promoted. He came rushing to thank me.

"Thanks a lot. Thank you, Sir. I have got it. You have done it. I will never forget what you have done for me." He was pumped up and was unable to control his emotions. He was shaking my hand, holding tightly to my hand within his hands.

"Kulshrestha Ji, I have not done any favour to you. I just wanted to teach you a lesson. Now you are an executive. You have no backing from the labour union. Now, I will hang you upside down and get all the work done. You will not be able to complain to anyone. Welcome to the world of executives." I laughed loudly to scare him.

"No problem, Sir. It will always be my pleasure." Kulshrestha Ji was shaking with joy. The pleasure of getting something after losing all hope is unparalleled. The news of the promotion spread all over the factory like fire. Arya Ji joined us. He was in high spirits. He was convinced that he was next in the queue. He would be in the same boat next year. He hugged Kulshrestha Ji joyfully and shook hands with me with great zeal.

Time was flying by, and everything was going well when, one day, an operator came to my cabin and informed me about another operator in our section who had been working secretly for some time to fabricate a pistol. Making a part for private purposes was not a big deal, but this was beyond imagination and could not be ignored. I discussed it with the supervisors and asked them to keep me informed so I could catch him red-handed with the unauthorised parts.

Later, I got a tip from the operator who had initially informed me. I waited a few minutes as he left my cabin and then casually walked towards the other operator. I was just a few steps away when the operator picked up the parts and fled towards his locker. By the time I reached his locker, he had gone from there. The supervisors came to help me. I requested the master key from the store so we could open his locker. We could not find anything in the locker. By now, the operator knew that I had become aware of the situation. Instead of placing the part in his locker, he had removed all the items in a split second. I requested the supervisors to inform the operator to see me.

After about fifteen minutes of the event, I was in my cabin when the operator entered. I asked him to take a seat.

"Tell me honestly what you were doing. I will try my best to help you. Otherwise, you will be on your own," I said in a firm but comforting tone.

"I was making some parts for my own use," the operator said without hesitation. He was sitting firm and had minimal expressions on his face.

"What are these parts for, and what will you do with them?" I sought a further explanation.

"I am making a pistol, and these parts will be used in it." The operator was not hiding anything from me and was blatantly honest, knowing precisely what this would lead to.

"This is the last time you have used the word 'pistol'. Now, do me a favour. Please draw the sketches of some of the parts that you have made and add a note that you have made these parts for your private use without the permission of your supervisors. Put the date, your name, and your signature at the end." I took a notebook from the drawer and handed it to him along with a pen. He quickly made three sketches, added the notes, signed the document, and handed it to me.

"Thank you for your cooperation. I have to submit this for further inquiry. You know that there will be disciplinary action against you. I will try my best so that you do not lose your job. You can go now." I tried to be as normal as I could be. I was trying to comprehend the whole situation. I was not expecting a confession so easily. I had no evidence or witnesses, yet now I had a strong case. Would the management agree to my recommendations to keep him at the job? Probably, the operator had handed over all his stress to me. I was confused and shaken.

As this case was sensitive, it went to the Chief of Administration, Col Malhotra, a retired Army executive. During the inquiry, the case was leaked to a reputed Newspaper, where Col Malhotra was targeted as if he was also involved in the illegal activities in the Tool Room section of Bharat Electronics Ghaziabad. Col Malhotra called me into his office to discuss the case in detail.

"Have you seen the Newspapers about this case? These cowardly people are trying to stab me in the back. I have been in the army and faced bullets from the front. I have not turned away to show my back to the bullets. I will teach the News agency a lesson. I have filed a defamation case against it and may need your help. I have looked at the sketches made by the operator. These are certainly the parts of a pistol. If you need any support, do not hesitate to contact me. We have your back."

Col Malhotra was angry and his voice sounded as if he was preparing for battle. He was a tall and handsome person. He limped a little. Most likely, his leg was injured by a bullet. He had a big office right next to the office of the Executive Director in an out-of-bounds, premium, red-carpeted area. This was my first visit to this part of the factory, which was a bit overwhelming.

"I am sorry, Sir. You are in trouble because of me. Let me know whatever help you need. I will try my best." I gathered all the courage to speak in front of an impressive personality.

"No, no, no. You have done the right thing and taken a courageous step. It is now my turn to set things right. Let me know, young man, if you need my support." Col Malhotra showed complete respect for me.

"Sir, I have promised the operator that he will not lose his job in return for his cooperation and honest confession since I did not have any evidence or witness against him." I lodged my request in the shortest possible words.

"I have no personal grudge against this employee. I will use my resources to find out who leaked this information to the Newspaper. Be in touch." Col Malhotra completed the conversation. I thanked him and left his chamber. A few months later, the court favoured Col Malhotra. He received a handsome amount as compensation from the News agency. The operator did not lose his job, but he lost all his seniority and had to start afresh. It was a big learning curve for me as well. I survived.

17. BE OFFICERS' COLONY

I was allocated a flat in the BE Executive Colony, a gated community. The surroundings were vibrant, as everyone in the colony worked for the same company and shared similar economic backgrounds, age groups, and intelligence levels. Manu found good company within his age group, while thoroughly enjoying the playground. In the evenings, the three of us would stroll around the playground, and Manu relished walking with us. He had a remarkable memory of the roads. Our neighbours, Prashant and his wife Sundaram, were a lovely couple around the same age as us. They had a son, Tunnu, who was in Manu's age group. Initially quite reserved, they eventually became very friendly with us. True to her name, Sundaram was a lovely and talented singer, while Prashant could also sing well, though he was not a trained singer like his wife.

BE Officer's Club was a good small organisation. The president and the secretary were usually elected from the executives living within the colony. Their main task was to organise cultural activities to help build friendships among the executives and their family members. Celebrating New Year was a big attraction, and executives from outside the colony were also invited. Safety and security were not a concern. Kids would play freely in the playground. We were no longer required to appoint a guard in the house during holidays while visiting our families.

We were having an excellent time as it was as close as possible to hostel life. One day, Shalu complained of a painful boil under her chin that was not subsiding. We visited a local doctor who gave us some medicines, but they proved ineffective. The doctor referred us to a senior doctor, Dr Dave, in a nearby hospital in Delhi, Walia Nursing Home. By this time, the boil had become larger and more painful. Dr Dave engaged the surgeon, Dr Sood, to operate on the lump and get a biopsy done. Shalu was hospitalised for the procedure. Dr Sood cut about two centimetres along the boil and then left it open. We were shocked by this procedure. How come the wound was left open? How would it heal? This would be tremendously painful. That evening, I was sitting in Dr Dave's chamber to get my head around such a procedure.

"Why is the wound not sealed after the operation? What is it?" I asked.

"It must be left open to keep the bad fluid coming out. She has a chronic disease." Dr Dave was familiar to us. He was the leading doctor in this nursing home. Earlier, we had spoken to him a few times during Manu's hospitalisation.

"What does that mean?" I asked the doctor. I had never heard the term chronic.

"A chronic disease goes on with the patient until their death. There are three chronic diseases: Cancer, AIDS, and TB. The biopsy report will take about two weeks. I am going to start treatment for TB. You pray to God that the biopsy report comes in favour of TB." Dr Dave provided me with a much-needed explanation.

"Why TB, doctor?" I was still confused.

"TB is the only disease out of the three which is curable with treatment." Dr Dave replied.

"What is the difference between cure and treatment?" Once again, English was not my forte, especially regarding technical aspects.

"Treatment is just about managing a disease. You have to be on medication for the rest of your life. On the other hand, a cure completely eliminates the disease after treatment. You can take her home and visit us every second day for the dressing." Dr Dave was not annoyed with my stupid questions. I was still trying to digest the difference.

Back home, I told Shalu about my conversation with Dr Dave. She asked me to inform her parents as we would need their help. It was going to be a long battle. Manu was young, and managing the office and home was hard for me. Shalu's mother joined us in a week. Shalu now also had high fever. I also informed my parents. Dr Dave dressed the wounds. He would first press firmly around the wound to get as much fluid out as possible and then insert medicine in powder form into the wound. This was an excruciating procedure for all of us: the doctor, me and, of course, Shalu. Shalu was brave. She was a fighter.

One morning, Shalu told me about a bad dream that she had.

"I had a bad dream last night. An ugly-looking, strong, tall man came to me. He held a pot filled with a thick black liquid in his hand. He grabbed me with his other hand and started force-feeding it into my mouth down my throat. He laughed wickedly and shouted from time to time: Have more. I am so scared. It was so real. I can still feel it." Shalu was horrified. I hugged her and tried to console her.

We were still waiting for the biopsy report when Shalu developed a second lump in her neck. It was growing fast and was also painful. Shalu was hospitalised again for an operation. Once again, the cut was left open after the lump was removed and sent for biopsy. Shalu was in the hospital for observation. She was deteriorating fast. She was not able to take in food and was throwing up in quick succession. This put tremendous stress on the wounds and made it unbearable for her. She looked into my eyes but did not speak. I could read her expression without any difficulties:

"*Please save me. I do not want to die. Manu is too young.*" She was gathering every ounce of courage and hope and was putting up a tough fight. I could only stick around her and touch her forehead occasionally. Shalu's mother and Manu also visited her and did their best to keep their chin up and provide her the much-needed encouragement. The biopsy report had come positive for TB. Shalu had TB in her lymph nodes. Our whole body is full of lymph nodes.

Though this was a significant relief for all of us, the current situation was not looking good. After three nights in the hospital, Shalu was discharged. Dr Dave trained me to do temporary dressings. Proper dressing was required every third day. Shalu was recovering slowly. It was more of a mental recovery than a physical one. She was getting the much-needed comfort from her mother's presence.

Now, it was my turn to dream. Three people engaged me in a street fight in the dark. Of the three, two were of the same build as me and were covered in black clothes and hoodies, thus making it hard for me to see their faces and guess their moves. The third one looked like their boss. He did not have many clothes on his body. He was tall, well-built, and muscular. He had two little horns on his head. His face was ugly and had deep spots as if left by smallpox. He had two tiny wings that helped him in lifting his body in the air. In short, he was the Devil. I was having a tough time fighting them, but suddenly, I did a great combo move. I struck the two men with my fist and turned around to kick the Devil with full strength from my stretched toe. *Khiyaaaaaa!* The battle was over. The three were on the ground and were not able to get up. I walked away safely. The dream did not make much sense until about a month later when Shalu developed a third lump, which also grew fast. Dr Dave arranged for this to be operated on, and Shalu was hospitalised again. This time I was calm. I assured Shalu that this would be the last operation to remove the infected lymph node, and after this, she would start recovering fast.

Shalu spent another three nights in the hospital, which was much better than the previous times. Dr Sood was not keen to do this operation and warned that Shalu might be unable to straighten her neck. This was due to the cluster of nerves that are present near the third lump. I discussed this with Dr Dave, who assured me that this would not be the case. Sometimes, surgeons have their own way of expressing things, which is short and crude. Though now, Shalu had three open wounds, she was somehow able to cope.

The second biopsy confirmed the previous results. The medicines were making a difference. The dressing continued for another two months. My parents also joined us and stayed for about three weeks. My doctor uncle also paid a two-day visit. He was a TB specialist. As TB is a contagious disease, my parents and uncle were worried about my health. However, Dr Dave assured us that this type of TB is not infectious. Shalu developed a fourth boil about a month after the third one, but it did not require any further attention and subsided by itself.

Shalu had survived. The three of us – Shalu, Manu, and I – were now closer than ever. We were paying monthly visits to Dr Dave. We were extremely thankful to him. He was popular and well-respected in that area. He used to come to the hospital in the morning around 9:00 am and could be seen surrounded by patients till 11:00 pm at night. Once, I asked him:

"Doctor, why did Shalu get TB despite immunisation in childhood?"

"Immunisation is not a guarantee against the disease. Look at our surroundings. There is so much garbage and clutter around us. All this leads to various diseases. As long as our body can fight these, we are fine. It is just a game of tug of war." Dr Dave explained.

"Yes, I never looked at it this way." I nodded my head in affirmation. Today, when I compare Australia with India, I can differentiate the approach in the cultural and social structure. Australia has one of the highest tax rates in the world, but then the money goes into building beautiful roads, footpaths, parks, schools, reliable infrastructure services like water, gas, electricity, communication, garbage removal, and above all, fundamental services like social security. There are excellent government hospitals that are necessary for a healthy and progressive generation. Though this upfront cost looks exorbitant, in the long run, it beats the ongoing cost of firefighting. It produces people who take pride in their work, whether cleaning public toilets or running an organisation as the CEO or head of the state. They pick up their pets' droppings when taking them for a walk. The gardens, parks, and shopping centres are clean after people visit them as they do not leave their litter around. The police are not there to scare people but to help them.

"I am still intrigued about the source. This disease runs in the family." Dr Dave added. He was not done with his investigation and, as a true professional, wanted to reach the root cause of the issue. He was right.

It had been about seven months since the treatment started, and Shalu had been doing all her home duties as usual, but her mother was not keeping well. She was getting weak due to excessive bleeding during her monthly cycles. We took her to Dr Dave, and after investigations, she was found positive for TB. The treatment did the trick for her as well, and she gained back her vitality.

Shalu's mother, Saroj Ji, was ready for the next challenge. The search was on for her second daughter-in-law for the eligible bachelor Sharad Kumar Saxena, Advocate – Etah, the second son and, more appropriately, Shalu's caretaker. Saroj Ji had received a lead from the husband of Sharad Ji's friend's sister. Bakul's uncle was his colleague. After a meeting the deal was sealed.

It had been over eighteen months since Shalu was on treatment for TB. Though initially, Dr Dave told us that the medication would last for about a year, for some reason, he had not stopped it. As per him, the growth of lymph nodes was way faster than cancer, and Shalu had had a very narrow escape. He was not prepared to take any chances. Though these medicines would have some side effects later in life, especially bone-related deficiencies, the priority was evident for now. I asked Dr Dave a few times about when he was going to stop the medication, but every time, he had assured us that he would do so in a month or two. The visit for this month was a special one.

"Doctor, I think Shalu is pregnant." I was a bit shy about opening my mouth. Had I put Shalu in trouble?

"That's great news," Dr Dave said, leaning back in his chair, taking both hands behind his head, stretching his upper body to provide much-needed relaxation, and continued:

"Let us stop all the treatment. The body has clearly stated that it has recovered and wants to lead a normal life. She does not need any support now. I will brief Dr Rukmani, the Gynaecologist at this hospital, on your case. She is an excellent lady. She will take good care of you." He scribbled on his letter pad and handed it to us.

We were fortunate to see Dr Rukmani that same day. She recommended several blood tests and offered general advice on diet and exercise. We felt relieved by Dr Dave's advice and were pleased to meet another competent lady doctor. The pregnancy was confirmed, and we visited Dr Rukmani regularly.

It had been about six months since Shalu was expecting. One day, she revealed her fear to me:

"I cannot sleep properly. I consistently have nightmares. I find ghosts in my dreams every night. This has been going on for the last two months. When I am awake, the baby kicks me so hard that I cannot stand it. I am scared about the baby. I am not sure if I am carrying a bad soul." Shalu was confused. Her big eyes were moist.

Her dreams had mostly manifested in some shape or form. What message were these dreams leading to? I was in deep thought. After a few moments, I broke the silence.

"I know this baby is a girl, a beautiful girl. She is playing with you. I am trying to figure out who the goddess of mysticism is." I was confident in my answer.

"You are indicating towards Goddess Lakshmi. She is also known as *Maya*, meaning illusion. The ghosts are more illusions than something real," Shalu replied. Unlike me, she was a religious girl who was keenly interested in stories about Gods and Goddesses.

"True, but we need a beautiful name for Goddess Lakshmi or *Maya*. Your God Shiva also likes the company of ghosts and horrible creatures. You have been fasting for him every Monday. I am confident he has something to do with this. The baby girl is a part of Lord Shiva." I was firm on my ground.

"Then what about we name her Shivangi?" I was amazed at how quickly and precisely Shalu had invented a new name that had never been heard before. Shivangi means the part of Shiva that has manifested as a girl. It sounded perfect. Among all the Gods, I appreciated Lord Shiva the most for his simplicity and impartial behaviour towards everyone, good or bad, rich or poor, ugly or beautiful, man or woman, human or animal.

"Shivangi, the most beautiful girl in this universe," I exclaimed joyfully and hugged Shalu.

"She also likes her name. I had a gentle hit in my belly." Shalu was filled with joy. Her face was shining. Her eyes shed small tears, which soon flooded with larger ones that she could not contain for long.

"Shivangi will be her official name, and her nickname will remain Ninni," I said enthusiastically. We had already decided on the name Ninni. It was a character in a TV serial that was based on a historical story which we had watched some time back. It was about the bold and beautiful daughter of a jungle tribe leader who became a princess and was renowned for her wisdom.

We told Manu that the baby will be his younger sister. She is wonderful and was coming exclusively for him. From that day, Shalu did not have any bad dreams. The baby and we were happy, but the happiest person in our family was Manu. He was impatient to meet his little sister, the most beautiful girl in the universe, Ninni, Shivangi.

Time was passing by. Shalu was eight months pregnant. I had not mentioned Shalu's pregnancy to anyone in my family as we wanted to surprise them. However, her parents learned about it due to my extra care and caution towards Shalu during a visit to Parmesh Sadan. My elder brother, Ajay Ji, visited us in March, around Manu's birthday, and stayed with us for a couple of days, but he did not notice the pregnancy. It was April, the delivery was due in mid-May, and Shalu's mom was ready to join us and help us. One day, I was telling Shalu about my dream that morning:

"I met Ninni today. She appeared in my dream. She looked like a teenager. She was tall, fair, of average build, and stunning. She seemed happy and was telling me something, but I cannot recall what it was. Her hair was curly, styled in many small knots, similar to Gautam Buddha's or that of some African people. I cannot wait to meet her; she is so beautiful." My heart was racing with excitement. I held Shalu tightly in my arms.

The ninth month had just started. Shalu told me about her contractions. I took her to Walia Nursing Home for a checkup. After inspection, Dr Rukmani told us that she was expecting the delivery that day, and Shalu needed to be admitted. It was close to afternoon. Shalu was taken into the labour room as her contractions had become frequent. The nurses were waiting for Dr Rukmani, who was extra busy that day. A nurse approached, rushing to her chamber, and shouted:

"Now, Doctor."

Dr Rukmani rushed to the labour room. Manu and I were standing outside, waiting anxiously. She was just in time to catch Ninni in mid-air. Shivangi could not wait anymore. The clock clapped, hitting both its hands. It was sharp 12 O'clock. Time welcomed Shivangi, joining both its hands in the shape of Namaste. A nurse came out to inform us.

"It is a baby girl." She informed in a low tone.

I sat down on my knees to hug Manu. He could not hold his

joy. His face was shining. We got up and danced. We could not contain our emotions. Ninni/Shivangi had joined us. Our family was now complete. The hospital staff and nurses were confused. They had not seen someone celebrating the birth of a baby girl.

Dr Rukmani came out of the labour room after about fifteen minutes. She delivered the news officially:

"Congratulations. You have a daughter. Shalini is fine. The baby girl has mild jaundice, so we have to put her under special lights for a few hours. You can visit both in another fifteen minutes." She went back to her chamber to attend to the remaining patients.

Shalu was brought back to the room. The three of us were united and ecstatic to see each other. Mission accomplished. Manu and I were taken to the special ward to meet Ninni. She was in a tiny cot under bright lights. Her face was covered with a soft white towel. I slowly lifted the towel to see her face. To our surprise, Ninni's eyes were wide open under the towel. The bright lights were not bothering her at all. The light coming out of her eyes was probably brighter and more powerful. Her head had tiny knots of curly hair scattered around. After all, she was not an ordinary baby. She was Shivangi, who represented Lord Shiva. We kept looking at Shivangi for some time and then looked at each other.

"She is beautiful," I spoke softly.

"Yes. My little sister," Manu replied equally softly, trying to hold his emotions in check.

I gave this news to Shalu's parents in Parmesh Sadan from a PCO, which was just adjacent to the nursing home. Shalu's mother joined us the same day. I informed my parents about the good news in Lucknow. They were happy but confused. Why had Ajay Ji not noticed? How could Atul and Shalini make a baby in just one month? Could this have been a trick by Shivangi to hide herself while standing right in front? Nothing is impossible for Lord Shiva. We gave tips to all the staff and nurses and shared sweets among our friends in the BE Colony.

Our parenting style for Ninni was entirely different from Manu's. We were not concerned about disinfecting everything around her. We would wait a few days and try home remedies instead of rushing to a doctor. We enjoyed her more than merely caring for her. Manu shadowed her like a personal commando. None of my real siblings had a daughter, so I seized every opportunity to tease them. Just like Manu, Ninni developed a strong bond with me. She would be so relaxed in my arms that she would fall asleep in no time.

We had been in the BE colony for over three years and had a good friend circle. There were quite a few bachelors among them: a young security officer who was a retired Army captain, an accountant, and young engineers living in nearby localities who visited the BE Club frequently in the evening. This year, we decided to participate in the social activities and games organised by the Club. Khilnani was the secretary. Just a week before the start of the activities, I asked Khilnani.

"Why don't you hand over all the trophies to us?"

"Why is that?" Khilnani asked.

"They will be ours anyway. I am just making your job simple." I laughed.

"In that case, you must participate and win it." Khilnani tried to show me my place.

"No problem if this is what you wish for." I undermined his confidence.

True to my words, we did bag many prizes. Manu in fancy dress and poetry reading, Prashant and me, Shalu and Sundaram in duet song, and Shalu and me in the couple's games. Destiny was favouring our family. We had bagged most prices, if not all.

18. MEDICAL ELECTRONICS

A new division, Innovation and Diversification, was created at BE Ghaziabad to identify new opportunities, especially in the commercial sector. Mr Mathur was made the head. This was done to sideline Mr Mathur. This new division was tiny, and Mr Mathur handpicked one of his trusted managers, Mr Gulati, for special advice and me as a workhorse. Mr Gulati was designated the Manager of the Diversification department.

A small part of the Tool Design was relocated into this division to overcome specific bottlenecks in artworks that were required for the control panels that needed text and other markings after the painting process. I was made head of this Tool Design section. It had two drafting technicians. Tool Room was still under Mr Mathur, but I had nothing to do with it now.

The time for promotions for Arya Ji was due that week. He was anxious. He approached me and reminded me of my promise. I tried to convince him that I had no influence in the Tool Room, but he provided a counterargument that it was still under the same division and that Mr Mathur was still heading it. I should be able to approach him on a personal level. I also did not want Arya Ji to be left behind, so I approached Mr Mathur.

"Sir, I want to remind you about Mr Arya Ji. This is his last chance. You got Mr Kulshrestha Ji promoted last year."

"But he does not report to you now. Tool Room is not under you." Mr Mathur interrupted and tried to push me back.

"But, Sir, I promised to get him promoted this year." I was sticking to old values.

"Let me see if I can do anything." Mr Mathur asked me to leave him alone.

Mr Mathur held my promise, and Arya Ji got into the executive cadre. Once again, I had a narrow escape. I needed to understand my limitations. I get myself into deep trouble at every possible trap. I still cannot understand why I get into hot water while everyone around me goes with the flow and enjoys a good time. What is wrong with me? Is this my OCD (Obsessive Compulsive Disorder)?

Is this why I am socially unfit? Is this what my father was always trying to teach me? Is this why I score so low on all the scales of a normal society? Even worse, have I passed this defective gene to my kids? Why does Shalu not point out this flaw? Is she also carrying a similar gene?

Mr Mathur belonged to the old school and would not trust even a calculator. Therefore, Computers, for him, were the biggest evil in a modern office, though this was slowly changing. He handed over most of his work, which included making presentations for the Board of Directors. He relied on me, but since I could complete his work in time, he left things for the last moment. He was getting the impression that, with computers, one could do a year's work in one month, or one month's work in one week, or one week's work in one day, and one day's work in one hour.

Effectively, as far as he was concerned, a year's work could be done in an hour. One day, he handed over a whole lot of scribbles in the afternoon to prepare a PowerPoint presentation for a Board meeting in Bangalore. He was to fly the next day, so the work had to be finished the same day. I was stuck late in the office along with Mr Mathur. This was unusual, and Shalu got worried. She contacted our friend Kashyap, the Security Officer in BE Colony. He jokingly assured Shalu that Johari must have stayed there for evening tea as he is very fond of the Bread Pakoras. However, he contacted the security staff at work to find out. Sunderam and Vidula, Shalu's friends who lived in the same block, gathered on our balcony to comfort her. That day, I reached home at least two hours late. As soon as I entered, Shalu threatened me in front of her friends:

"Get in. I will take your class." Shalu had a commanding tone.

"That's very good. Would you teach me the same way as you did yesterday? Let us get in quick?" My face was full of cheeky expressions. I grabbed Shalu softly by her left shoulder, pushed her closer, and started walking in. Shalu blushed. She could not respond. Sunderam and Vidula were stunned. They covered their mouths spontaneously and ran away, bursting into laughter.

"It is not my fault. You ask Mrs Mathur to set Mr Mathur right. He is my boss, but you can set him right through his boss." I was trying to plant the seed in Shalu's mind. Mr Mathur lived in a D-type flat in the BE Colony. After most of the males left for work, the ladies in the colony gathered in the park to gossip and to sit in the Sun.

Though the factory accommodation was excellent, it had a significant cost factor. We needed to pay 10% of our basic pay as rent, and we missed out on the Rent Assistance allowance, which was 30% of the basic salary. In total, I was down by 40% of my basic salary. Some smart people discovered a balancing formula for it. The company paid a car allowance. This was effective only for the executives living close to the factory as they could not avail company conveyance. This seemed a lucrative solution. I decided to buy a second-hand car. I had no upfront money, so I took a loan from the company.

As I knew very little about cars and the second-hand car market, I got help from a friend and bought a Fiat car. This turned out to be a bad deal. It took a lot of money for repairs and was still unreliable. After paying the loan instalment and for the repairs, there was not much money left to enjoy the car.

However, the car proved helpful to the Tingal family during Rani Didi's treatment. She was very sick and had come to us with her brothers and father for investigations. They stayed with us for about a week. Unfortunately, the doctors could not establish a precise diagnosis. We did our best to make their stay as comfortable as possible.

Since not much work was left in Tool Design, Mr Mathur transferred me to Medical Electronics. This was a new section. There was a joint venture at the national level to manufacture a LINAC machine. LINAC is an abbreviation for Linear Accelerator. The machine is used for radiotherapy in treating cancer patients. The organisations involved in this project were BHEL (Bharat Heavy Electricals Limited) in Haridwar, SAMEER (Society for Applied Microwave Electronics Engineering & Research) an offshoot of BARC (Bhabha Atomic Research Institute) in Bombay, CSIRO (Central Scientific Instruments Organisation), and PGI Medical College in Chandigarh that had most advanced facilities for cancer treatment in India at that time.

None of these organisations could produce the parts of the LINAC tube to the required precision, thus Mr Mathur offered the services of Bharat Electronics Ghaziabad. He had also proposed BE Ghaziabad facility for testing this machine by upgrading the existing NDT (Non-Destructive Testing) facility that was used to test the flaws of welded joints by using natural Cobalt 60 equipment.

There were quite a few challenges in producing the series of parts for the LINAC tube that would be joined at SAMEER through a unique process. I visited SAMEER Bombay and BHEL Haridwar to introduce myself, get acquainted with these organisations' roles, and get an idea of the project's progress. BHEL was making the Gantry for the machine. The Gantry was a metallic framework of the machine that would house all the components. BHEL had produced parts for the LINAC tube, but during the testing, they had failed miserably, though from the naked eye, these parts had looked perfect. At CSIRO Chandigarh, I witnessed the team's work on the Collimator which is used to shape the beam to match the formation of the cancerous part in the body. I also attended a couple of medical conferences and visited PGI Chandigarh, where the number of cancer patients inundated me. This opened my eyes to the significance of this project.

At BE Ghaziabad, I spent two months in producing parts of the LINAC tube by using aluminium metal for trials. Despite all the modern technology and hard work, I was not getting the parts right. I reached out to Mr Mathur for help. He asked me to bring all the notes and the results of the groundwork that I had done so far. I was sitting across his desk with the pile of papers that I had collected over the past two months. Mr Mathur was keenly going through my notes while rolling a few hairs of his moustache between his thumb and index finger. This was a sign of his extreme focus.

"You will never reach the Moon." Mr Mathur delivered the verdict in a bit of annoyance. This was the first time he had raised his voice at me.

"Pardon me, Sir," I uttered, not understanding his intentions.

"You cannot reach the Moon, Johari. You need to be a scientist to reach the Moon. They formulate their experiments very methodically. By doing this, they watch the impact of individual parameters on the process and then control the progress until they get full control with the desired results. You have acted just like an Engineer. There is no pattern. Everything is haphazard." Mr Mathur was still upset. Clearly, I had wasted two months.

"What do I do now?" I asked for guidance.

"There is a rule for understanding things. If you are trying to understand a big object like a building, you need to make a small model of it, and if you are trying to understand a small object, then you must make an enlarged model of it. In this case, we are trying to understand the cutting tool's minute movements and how they impact accuracy. So, let us draw a scaled-up version of the LINAC cavity and the various positions of the cutting tool within it."

After Mr Mathur explained the concepts to me, I refined the process and got the results within two weeks. I approached Mr Mathur and said:

"Sir, look at this plot from a 3D coordinate measuring machine. It is perfect within 20 microns all around." My heart was pumping with joy.

"Yes, that looks good. Well done." Mr Mathur looked at me as if saying, *"I am proud of you."*

"Sir, I want to share something with you." I requested.

"Go ahead." Mr Mathur was in a good mood.

"You have always motivated, encouraged, guided, and appreciated my work, but I was always scared. Until last year, I used to regularly get bad dreams that I had failed in the final exams of engineering. I would wake up drenched in sweat and fear. I would look around to find Shalu, Manu, and Ninni to regain my breath." I shared my secret with Mr Mathur.

"So, your bad dreams are over. I still get these bad dreams." Mr Mathur looked puzzled while sharing his similar trauma.

I provided enough machined LINAC cavities to SAMEER Bombay to produce and test a LINAC tube in the lab. The results were encouraging, but the ordeal was not yet over. The testing facility at BE Ghaziabad needed funding approval from Mr Gupta, ED (Executive Director), the head of the three units of Bharat Electronics in Northern India. Mr Gupta was known to be a furious executive, and it was against his status to speak to an executive below the level of senior manager. The amount involved in upgrading the NDT facility was significant, and the stakes were high. Would the machine fit in the room and rotate a full 360 degrees? The Gantry parts were so big that bringing them into the room through the gallery was a challenge. The entrance to this room was through a gallery which had been explicitly designed to avoid any radiation leaving the room.

I did computer simulations by using AutoCAD software. I was confident there would be just a two-plus centimetre of clearance between the roof and the machine head in a vertical position. I also traced the exact way to get the largest part of the Gantry into the room. It had to be done by driving the trailer into reverse position to maximise the turning radius.

My Manager, Mr Jain, and the DGM, Mr Mathur tried to convince the ED, Mr Gupta, but he was not ready to take any chances. He wanted to have a personal meeting only with me. Mr Jain delivered the bad news to me. A meeting of a Senior Engineer with the Executive Director was nothing short of a meeting between the rabbit and the lion in the famous children's story. The next day, I was in Mr Gupta's cabin, all by myself.

"Sir, you wanted to see me?" I asked politely. His slightly deformed face made him look even more dangerous. He had survived a bad car accident, which had left a big scar on his left cheek.

"So, you are confident the machine will fit into the room. Is that correct?" Mr Gupta looked penetratingly into my eyes.

"Yes Sir, I have done computer simulations. The clearance is just over 2-centimetres." I said confidently.

"If you are proven wrong, be prepared for my wrath. I will not leave you." He threatened me.

"I am confident, Sir, that the machine will fit into the room and will be able to take a full rotation without hitting the roof." I was polite but firm in my tone.

"Okay, you can go now. I will approve the funding, but remember what I have told you." Mr Gupta warned me.

"Thank you very much, Sir. You will not be disappointed." I left the room.

In another few months, the testing facility was ready. Gantry parts arrived. My theory proved correct. The trolley operator could get the parts in by driving in the reverse direction. The parts were assembled. There was a clear gap between the roof and the Gantry in an upright position. I had survived once again, though this time just by two centimetres.

PART 4
THE FAMILY

19. MIGRATION TO AUSTRALIA

We were having a great time. Our family was complete. We had a son and a daughter with a perfect age difference of five years. Our friend circle was fantastic. It had people from different professions and ages. We were well respected, and some of the younger engineers from my institute used to greet Shalu by touching her feet. Our gathering was full of fun. People around us wondered if we had some life-secrets and were somewhat envious of us. Within our family unit, we were four, but we were just one for everyone else. We had established our place in Shalu's extended family and were loved and respected by all.

However, we were left loose by my family and were drifting away from them. After all, I had disappointed my parents not once but a few times. I was outspoken and had very different perception and values. On the contrary, Abhay Ji, my elder brother, was working hard to meet the expectations of our parents. He was caring and respectful of them while being worldly-wise. He had established himself as a true successor of my father, the Great Lion King.

But it seemed as if this was not enough, because life was getting ready to play another role in our lives. I had not followed the rule of the jungle and had left the herd. I was vulnerable, and so was my family unit. Inflation was increasing at a fast pace. India was going through a recession. Salaries had not kept pace with the inflation. The gap had grown so much that halfway through the month we would have no money. I applied for jobs in the private sector but did not have much luck.

Shalu also approached a few schools but could not get a teaching position. We tried the retail business of ladies' garments from our house, but being within a gated colony it was not the ideal situation. I attempted tutoring children, but it was not worth the effort, and once again, being in a gated colony was not the best opportunity. I was not tuned in and so missed some early housing committees that could have changed our destiny within two to three years. When I finally invested in a housing committee, it proved to be an absolute dud.

I felt surrounded by shadows and darkness. I often dreamed of standing on a railway track in a narrow tunnel with no escape and two trains approaching fast from both ends. I shared my frequent bad dreams with Shalu. My car was unreliable, and travelling with four people on a scooter was risky. Road accidents were common in India. Due to fear of the police and litigations, no one would come to help, leaving accident victims to die on the roads.

So far, my patriotism was holding me back, but it was inevitable that I would no longer have a place in India. Every year, five to ten engineers from our company migrated to Australia. Recently, Kamarjit told me that his application for migration was also in the advanced stage and hopefully, he would soon get good news.

One day, we were driving back to our home on the scooter. I decided to stop at a shopping strip close to our house.

"Why did you stop here?" Shalu asked as she got down from the scooter, holding Ninni in her arms. Manu had already stepped down from the front of the scooter and was looking at Ninni.

"I am left with just Rupees 12 in my wallet. Today is only the 21st of the month. This will not be much help for the rest of the month, so I have decided that all of us will have *Paani Puri* and spend this money as well." I replied in a flat tone. By now, Ninni was standing on the ground, holding Manu's hand.

"Yes, we are going to have Paani Puri," Manu told Ninni, who was also smiling, infected by Manu's big smile.

We all had Paani Puri; for Ninni, we got it with sweet *Chutney*. We were left with no money and no false hope.

"What is your plan now?" Shalu asked as we approached our scooter.

"I am going to apply for migration to Australia." My voice was firm. I knew this would be painful for Shalu as she was close to her family. She was very emotional, and there had hardly been a day since our marriage when she had not referred to her parents or brothers or cousin brothers and sisters or Parmesh Sadan in our discussions. The thought of leaving the country was more devastating for her than any misfortune. She had bravely overcome her battle with TB, but this was much worse, living without her life.

A life is defined by loved ones. A life simply means to love and to be loved. Now, she had to slice her heart into two. She had to take her family unit, leaving everyone else behind. Everything would just be a memory, a thing of the past.

I did not know how to apply for migration to Australia. So, the very next day, I contacted Kamarjit and asked him about it.

"It is good that you have decided now." Kamarjit explained the process enthusiastically. He was a man of few words, and I did not expect such an elaborate explanation. Due to our good relations and friendship, he looked happy about my decision.

I worked methodically to get my migration application right. It was not easy to complete all the documentation and get all the certificates. When it was not possible to get a required document, I had to make an affidavit and get it authorised by the approved authorities. Luckily, some executives from the Department of Defence were stationed in our factory and they could authorise.

Though I tried to keep the process secret, the distinct yellow colour envelopes used by the Australian embassy and the tendency to peek at the neighbour's mailbox before picking up their own mail could not keep it a secret for long. It had already been over six months, and the biggest hurdle was over.

My engineering degree was accepted. I was not required to appear in the technical exam, but I had to qualify the English test. I had responded to the embassy, clarifying that all my graduation studies and the work in the factory involved the English language, but my argument was dismissed. I must have made enough grammar and spelling mistakes in my application, so the Australian Embassy wanted to ensure my language competency. The test had two parts: written and oral. Shalu was not required to pass these tests. Being the principal applicant, I had to score high grades to qualify. How embarrassing it would be if I could not qualify this hurdle; just the thought of it made me feel terrible. English had never been my forte. The next few months were hard for me, though I did not let it become apparent.

As our migration application progressed, we decided to spend some time at Parmesh Sadan so Shalu could enjoy time with her family. I had always treated Shalu's younger cousins well. This time, they wished to oblige me. Chunmun, the eldest of the cousin brothers at Parmesh Sadan, approached me:

"Jija Ji, I want to give you a treat." I was impressed by the initiative.

"What is your plan, Chunmun?" My tone encouraged him.

"We will organise a party for you. You are special to us," Chunmun replied. I was amazed by his thoughtfulness. He was too young to think like this.

"Good idea. If you do not mind, can I take over from here and make it a unique party for everyone at Parmesh Sadan?" I offered.

"Yes, sure, but I would also like to contribute." Chunmun did not want to drop his responsibilities.

"Everyone in Parmesh Sadan and at Tingal's will have to participate and play their role. All the cooking must be done by the males, without any help or even consultation from any female. It will be a dinner party, and the only thing expected from the females to dress up for the occasion. They will be treated as chief guests, and the boys will serve them. What do you think?" I elaborated on my spontaneous plan and sought his opinion.

"That sounds good. I will let everyone know. When do you want to have the party?" Chunmun was excited.

"Coming Friday. That will give us a few days to prepare. I will talk to each family member's head to decide what dish to cook. Everything will be prepared within the house, which includes snacks. You kids can also decide if you want to come up with any quick and easy dish. I will need all the kids to be dressed in their best and ensure that all the ladies are served at their seats, even a glass of water." I summed up.

"Done." Chunmun's eyes were shining. He had got the central role. He was my right hand.

By the following day, Chunmun had spread the idea around. Everyone was excited but confused. No male member had any cooking skills. In India, at that time, most males were spoiled, first by their mothers and then by their wives. They knew no household skills like cleaning, washing, or doing the dishes. Cooking was not even in their books. The condition that they could not even consult any female member was too stringent, but I purposefully imposed this. I promised my full support for cooking. After all, post marriage, I had provided Shalu with the initial vital lessons on cooking and was a *Guru* among an ignorant crowd.

Friday came. It was the 1st of April. The Tingals were convinced that this was just a hoax, which is why this date was chosen. It turned out that it was also Illa uncle's birthday that day. He was overexcited about the whole concept. He was also proud of his cooking skills as he sometimes cooked non-vegetarian dishes. He decided to take responsibility for three dishes. Stuffed eggplant, stuffed tomatoes, and a sweet dish.

On the day of the event, he got up early in the morning to ensure that he had plenty of everything. When I visited him in the morning, he was sitting on the ground in the family room right in front of his kitchen. Around him were some 25 eggplants, 40 tomatoes, 4-kg onions, ½-kg garlic, 2-kg Desi Ghee, 6-litres of milk, 3 knives, a chopping board, a few big pots, and some 10 different spices.

"Happy Birthday, Illa uncle. Do you need any help? You have taken too much on yourself. Just one dish was enough." I was overwhelmed by his initiative and preparedness.

"Thank you, Atul Ji. I will be fine. I enjoy cooking, and you all will have the chance to appreciate my preparations today." Illa uncle replied. His eyes were shining, and as he laughed lightly, his belly moved synchronously.

"I am sure everyone will love your dishes. I will be around if you need a hand. Just one request, Illa uncle, as Suman aunty abstains from onion and garlic, please take out a portion of the dishes before you mix the onion and garlic?" I responded.

"Sure, that is no problem at all. When preparing the stuffing, I will fry the onion and garlic paste separately from the other spices." Illa uncle looked in total control.

Next in my line was Ravindra Kumar, Shalu's dad. He stood close to the kitchen, both hands locked behind his back, looking up at the highest shelf.

"What have you decided for today, Papa Ji?" I hesitantly called him Papa Ji. I struggled to call Shalu's parents, Papa Ji and Mummy Ji, while Shalu had no trouble addressing mine in a similar manner. Why was it hard for me? Shalu's mom had complained that I never called her Maa, though I did occasionally address Shalu's dad as Papa Ji.

"I am going to make *Panch Tatvi Daal*." Ravindra Kumar replied in a mystic tone.

"What is that?" I asked curiously, though I had some idea about his intention.

"Our body comprises five basic elements: Earth, Water, Air, Fire, and Space. I will mix five different types of lentils to make the *Daal*. I need 1-kg each of five yellow lentils." He answered.

"1-kg each of the raw lentil? You mean a total of 5-kg? Are you going to feed the whole city?" I almost screamed in shock and continued:

"You need only ½-kg of the raw lentils in total." I was frightened by his sense of measurement.

"No chance. I need at least a kilo of each lentil." Shalu's dad insisted.

"I need to get the ladies of the house involved now. It is an emergency. Shalu, come here and bring your mom along." I spoke loudly so I could reach out to Shalu.

"What is the matter?" Shalu asked. Her mother was also standing next to her.

"Your dad wants to make *Panch Tatvi Daal* and needs 1-kg of each raw lentil. Please tell him that he only needs ½-kg of the mix. I am breaking my rule by consulting with you people." I sought the help of the ladies to avoid a disaster. After much persuasion, the deal was settled at 200 grams of each lentil. I arranged five yellow lentils from three kitchens in Parmesh Sadan and moved to Bhaiya uncle to check his progress.

"Hello, Bhaiya uncle. How are you? What are you cooking for tonight?" I caught up with Bhaiya uncle on the veranda outside his room.

"I will arrange for the drinks. I will get the soda water bottles and pouches of Rasna powder. When mixed in the soda water, it forms a much better drink than the ones you see in the market."

Bhaiya uncle looked more interested in taking responsibility for the drinks rather than the dinner itself.

"Wonderful. Please let me know if you change your plan or need my help." I stayed with him for another fifteen minutes and came back to the kitchen to check on how the preparation of the *Daal* was going. Shalu's dad stood in the kitchen, staring at the gas stove.

"It is not going to lighten up by your Yogic power. You need a lighter." I picked up the lighter from the shelf, rotated the gas knob and clicked the lighter to generate the spark to turn on the gas stove. Shalu's dad's face started glowing and he was now looking brighter than the burner. One more hurdle was over. He had never turned on a gas stove in his life before.

"I have taken exactly 200 grams each and mixed them well. I washed them five times, so no dust, artificial colour, or coating is left. I know I need to boil it, but I am unsure how much water I need to add or which utensil is suitable for boiling." Shalu's dad was in high spirits.

"A pressure cooker would be the best. You need to add 5 to 6 times water. You must also add salt and some turmeric powder to get the colour. After the first whistle from the pressure cooker, turn the gas flame to low by turning this knob. After another two whistles, turn off the gas and leave it to cool down. We will taste it for salt and add Desi Ghee and some spices to enhance the taste. I will be around. Just call me when you need help." I did not want to stand beside him and take away his pride. He was ready to take off on the flight to the moon.

Another hour passed, and it was about 11 am. Babbi Dada arrived from Shalu's Bua's place. He was confident that this event was a hoax but he wanted to be sure. He was shocked to see the progress and the entire environment.

"Atul Bhai, Namaste. Is the event happening? Is it all real? I thought you were making April Fool of us. We have lost time. We need to catch up. Sorry for misjudging. I am going back right now and will get everyone into action." Babbi Dada was shocked and confused, trying to rush.

"Namaste, Babbi Dada. You still have a lot of time. We plan to assemble around 5 pm. What will you be cooking?"

"Mammi Ji used to roast a full cauliflower in spices. It tasted excellent. We will decide on one more dish and be here by 5 pm." Babbi Dada stammered under pressure.

"Fantastic, Babbi Dada. Can you please remove a portion of the dishes before adding onion and garlic so that Suman aunty can also enjoy them?"

"Sure, no problems. Bye, Atul Bhai. See you in the evening." Babbi Dada rushed back without seeing anyone else.

It was 3:00 pm. I was standing in the veranda, getting ready for another round of inspection. Chunmun and his younger brother, Dabbal, entered Parmesh Sadan from the back entrance, which connected to the rear portion of the side gallery. This was the main entrance for Bhaiya uncle and Suman aunty's family, as their portion had no opening in the front section. Dabbal was carrying a big bag.

"Hello, Chunmun and Dabbal; where are you coming from?" I asked curiously.

"I am coming from Bua's home. Babbi Dada and Sanjay Dada are busy cooking. Even Phoopha Ji is helping them in the kitchen. They are preparing roast cauliflower and *Dum Aloo*. Both the Bhabhi Ji's were teasing them as this was the first time that the two brothers worked in the kitchen. Hopefully, they will get things ready in time." Chunmun replied.

He did not want to leave things till the last moment and sneaked in to confirm that the Tingals were working as per plan. Dum Aloo is an exotic curry recipe that is made of whole potatoes. The potatoes are peeled and fried in vegetable oil until they become pink. Then, they are cooked in a curry, which contains grounded nuts and cream.

"I have got Monaco biscuits, cheese, and cucumber. This will make a good snack to start with. In our army parties, they put a slice of cucumber and cheese on top of the Monaco biscuits to serve along with drinks." Dabbal, who had joined the Indian army, looked handsome.

"That is a great idea. I will get salted cashews and peanuts to go with the snacks. What time will Subhash uncle start making the *Imartis*? I want it as a sweet dish," I asked. Subhash Sweet Shop was one of the oldest sweet shops in Etah. This was the only shop that used pure Ghee in its preparations, making it very special. The shop's owner, Subhash Ji, was Suman aunty's family friend.

"If you go in about half an hour, it should be fine. Do you want me to come along?" Chunmun answered.

"No, it is not far. I will be fine. I have asked the helping lady to prepare the Chapatis in our kitchen. She will be coming around 6 pm. This way, the Chapatis will still be somewhat fresh. Can you guys cook plain rice?" I elaborated on my plan and asked for further help.

"That is easy. How much rice should be enough? Chunmun asked.

"Half a kilo should be sufficient," I answered.

As Chunmun and Dabbal disappeared into their kitchen, I started walking towards Illa Uncle's kitchen. His stuffed eggplants were in the final stage, but the tomatoes had yet to start. He was preparing to cook *Kheer*, a sweet dish made of rice and milk.

"Hello, Illa Uncle. It seems you have not had any breaks today. You look a little tired. Have you had lunch?" I asked.

"Stuffed vegetables took longer to cook. I underestimated the time." Illa uncle replied.

"You can leave the tomatoes. You need to rest for some time and then get ready. After all, you are the chief guest, the birthday boy. You should relax so you look your best. We will deal with these tomatoes tomorrow," I assured Illa Uncle.

It was about 5:30 pm. The kids had completed the seating arrangement in the courtyard. The table, chairs, and cots were nicely arranged. All the children were smartly dressed and ready to serve the guests. Bhaiya uncle and Ravindra Kumar had come out of their rooms and were received by Sonu, the youngest brother of Chunmun and Pintu, the youngest son of Bhaiya uncle. Both Bhaiya uncle and Ravindra Kumar were dressed smartly and had winning smiles. The ladies were preoccupied with adding final touches to their dresses, applying makeup, and checking one another for any imperfections.

"How are things? Do you need any help?" This was Shalu. She

approached me in the courtyard. She looked amazing. Though she was a little nervous, her excitement was clearly visible. Shalu had never spent too much time in getting dressed up.

"Check with your mom and aunties if they need your help in dressing up. The Tingals will be arriving soon. Everyone should be here before they arrive," I suggested.

Very soon, the rest of the Parmesh Sadan members had gathered in the courtyard. All the aunties and Shalu's mom, Saroj, looked gorgeous. They had selected their best saris and jewellery for the occasion. The whole environment was filled with excitement and everyone looked forward to some unexpected fun. As the Tingals arrived, the excitement and noise level skyrocketed. Everyone was greeting everyone.

Babbi Dada and Sanjay Dada were typical party people. Their sheer presence was sufficient to bring life to a party. It was just so hard for everyone to hide their enthusiasm. Sonu and Pintu were busy serving cold drinks. Dabbal was serving the snacks. The army dish was impressive. Dabbal had scored full marks. Chunmun focused on ensuring that everyone was being looked after. From time to time, Chunmun would come to check with me to see if everything was proceeding as planned.

I was amazed. Just a simple idea had touched so many people. The glory of Parmesh Sadan was once again alive. What turned this event into such an electric and enjoyable moment? Was it because the idea was brilliant, or did it touch everyone's heart, or did it involve everyone, or had everyone been waiting for such a moment? All it needed was just a spark because it seemed that the souls of Parmeshwari Dayal and Jagrani had come to bless the occasion.

My mind was unable to pinpoint any specific reason. Maybe we have unnecessarily complicated our lives. Maybe we have surrendered to our ego. Maybe we have grown up and stopped listening to our younger selves. Maybe we have completely stopped listening to our inner voices. Maybe we do not have enough courage to act on our ideas and are happy to kill ourselves every day.

"Atul Ji, only you could have made this possible." This comment brought me back to the party. This was Shalu's Phoopha Ji, Jagdish

Tingal, who had retired as DIG (Deputy Inspector General of Police), and who was the most respected person in the family.

"It was Chunmun's initiative. I just took over his idea, and everyone made it possible. I am told that you have cooked Dum Aloo." I tried to deflect the topic to hide my embarrassment.

"I just helped Sanjay. It is great to see everyone together in such high spirits. It reminds me of when I was at the job and used to come here. A lot has changed since then. How long are you here?" Jagdish uncle looked happy and relaxed.

"Yes, Shalu has told me about the golden era of this family. It is still here, or this could not have turned out so well. I will leave the day after tomorrow." As I was chatting with Jagdish uncle, my eyes caught sight of Saroj Ji. She was looking at us. Her eyes were moist, and she was trying to wipe away her tears. She was in a state of bliss. Shalu was standing a little further and watching us and her mom.

She approached her mom and hugged her. I could see that Saroj Ji was trying to say something, but she was overwhelmed by emotions. Somehow, she controlled herself from bursting into tears, she took Shalu's hand into her hands and nodded her head sideways as if wanting to say, "Nothing". No words were exchanged.

As Jagdish uncle moved on to join Ravindra Kumar, Shalu stole the opportunity to come close to me. She was trying to control her emotions as well. Her eyes were saying a lot. Her heartbeats complemented her feelings.

"I love you," Shalu murmured. I was drowned by the emotions. I was trying to say, "*I know you loved me from day one. You are my charm. I love you too*", but the words were stuck in my throat. I just kept looking at her. The time had frozen.

"Jija Ji, should we start serving dinner? It is past eight." Chunmun interrupted us.

"Sure, come with me," I replied, and we moved to the kitchen. The helping lady had finished making Chapatis and was heating the Daal.

All the boys started serving dinner. The ladies and gentlemen took their place around the table.

"Suman aunty, you will not be missing any dish. Especially for you, everyone has taken out a portion of their dish before mixing the onion and garlic. Let us know if we have passed the cooking test." I prepared her plate and wanted to ensure that she felt special.

"Everything is looking amazing. The aroma is exotic. I am sure it will taste wonderful. You all have taken so much pain for me." Suman aunty was ecstatic.

After most people had finished their dinner, I attracted everyone's attention:

"Let us wish Illa Uncle."

"Happy Birthday to you, Happy Birthday to you, Happy Birthday, Illa Uncle, Happy Birthday to you." The chorus filled the environment. Everyone gathered around Illa uncle, sitting on the cot with both hands raised and joined together to acknowledge the greetings.

The food was exceptional. The ladies passed on their praise to everyone who had cooked. The Sweets were being served. The occasion had turned into a festival. All reservations had melted away. Smiles were being exchanged. Everyone had made this possible.

Three months passed since our visit to Etah. My results of the English written test had come, and I had successfully qualified for the next round of viva tests which were to be held in a month. This was a big relief. The next month, I received a request to submit the medical examination certificate. There was a list of authorised doctors and clinics and an elaborate form to fill about our medical history. There were two sticky points. My blood sugar was borderline, and Shalu had a history of TB.

My friends advised me not to declare TB for Shalu, but I did not want to take any chances. The form had a clause written in bold that any false declaration would result in visa cancellation. This would be a disaster. I was dead against any false declaration and left the outcome to destiny. To everyone's surprise, the result came in our favour. We were granted a permanent visa on the condition that we would take a TB oath and undergo a medical examination within three months of arriving in Australia. We had about four to five months to complete the remaining formalities and reach Australia, or our visa would be cancelled.

The migration application process had taken over a year. During this time, we experienced helplessness, while waiting and watching, we went through anxiety, prayers, a game of hide and seek, and many other emotions. While all this concluded, another series of crises surrounded us. Where would the money come for buying the tickets and surviving for the first few months until we got a job or some social security assistance from the Australian government? Where would we stay? Would there be any jobs for us? How would we dispose our assets? What would we carry to Australia, and what would we leave in India? Would we survive there? If we survived, would we be able to visit our parents and siblings?

There was no turning point for us. We had come too far. Our friends congratulated us, and while some people felt envious, we remained nervous and frightened, unable to express our feelings. Manu was happy with the thought of settling into a new country. Ninni was too young to understand anything. Shalu was relying on me. I had no choice. I had to be brave, very brave. Our extended families had yet to understand that we were not going away for just a year or two but for good.

I had begun preparing for migration and was considering resigning when our company announced a Voluntary Retirement Scheme (VRS). This was the first time that the company had introduced such a scheme. Anyone who had completed ten years of service could apply for it. It was perfect timing. I had just finished ten years of service, and although this scheme was not particularly attractive financially, something was better than nothing. The big question was, why would I be granted voluntary retirement, as everyone knew that my migration application had been approved, and I would leave regardless?

The Voluntary Retirement Scheme required approval from my manager first, then my divisional head, followed by the head of administration, and finally by the CMD at the Bangalore unit. My manager, Mr R K Jain, and my divisional head, Mr A K Mathur, were very supportive. They approved my application, and now it was awaiting Col Malhotra's, head of the personnel and administration division, approval. I decided to meet him to explain my situation. I knew him since the Tool Room incident, where I had caught an operator making a revolver. My friends and well-wishers strongly opposed this idea; nevertheless, I felt I had to take a chance. I needed to stand firm with the truth.

Once again, I was in the out-of-bound, carpeted area on the top floor of the administrative building. I was sitting in front of Col Malhotra.

"Hello, young man. How are you? How can I help you?" Col Malhotra welcomed me warmly.

"How are you, Sir? I need a favour from you. I have applied for the Voluntary Retirement Scheme, and I would like my application to be considered." I spoke respectfully.

"But this scheme is for dead woods like me, not for a young man like you. You have a bright future in this organisation. We need daring people like you in our organisation." Col Malhotra responded enthusiastically.

"My application for migration to Australia has already been approved, and I will leave anyway. It will give me some financial help if I get voluntary retirement." I responded without adding any fluff. There was silence in the room for a few seconds.

"Ok, leave it to me." Col Malhotra responded in a deep voice.

"Thank you, Sir." I wished him and left the room. Col Malhotra was leaving for Bangalore the very next day.

After returning from Bangalore, he called me to his office.

"Good news, Johari. Your application has been approved." Col Malhotra delivered the message without any formalities.

"Thank you, Sir." I was relieved.

"You know, I obtained approval for all ten applicants from the Ghaziabad unit just because of you. Now, no one can accuse me of favouring you." Col Malhotra explained. His voice clearly showed that it was not an easy job. I had put him in a difficult position. He was not complaining. His eyes were shining as if he was saying, "Young man, anything for you."

"Thank you very much, Sir." I acknowledged and left the room.

20. THE LUCKY COUNTRY

The time for indecision was over. We were all set to move to Melbourne. Excitement was mixed with nervousness. Shalu was sad, but she knew we had no other option. Right then, there were other things to worry about. In each phone conversation with Kamarjit, he insisted that we stay with him for the initial period. He also advised us about clothing, utensils, and other essential things which we should bring. The biggest asset to be disposed of was the car. My youngest uncle agreed to buy it. That was a great relief. We left most of the furniture and the bigger items in Parmesh Sadan for Shalu's parents.

We cherished the three embroideries of human faces on a black cloth from Sikkim. We gifted one each to Shalu's parents, my parents, and my elder brother Abhay Ji as a memento. This was to ensure that they retain some of our sweet memories in case we never return. I left my favourite sketch that I had made in BHUIT with my parents. This showed how capital punishment was carried out by crushing the head of a victim with a massive elephant during the Mughal Empire in India. We were allowed to carry only limited weight to Australia, and this sketch alone carried much weight for me. I left all the mental and emotional baggage in India. I wanted to start afresh. It was rebirth for all of us.

As we were staying in a company house, we had to leave it before the company could settle our accounts and release me from their services. Shalu's younger brother, Annu, was staying with us while he was working in New Delhi. He also needed to shift. We found a one-room set near our colony and planned to move there. We understood that it would be challenging to remain there for an extended period due to space limitations, so we chose the date of retirement, which was merely a week before our departure.

Life is about continuous change. While we were busy disposing most of our belongings, we also shopped for new clothes, kitchen utensils, and big suitcases to carry everything. Being a one-way trip, we were allowed to carry 40-kg per person. We bought a soft toy for Ninni as she was leaving behind all her friends. Ninni named it

Chota, meaning baby. This was her new friend who would migrate with her. Manu was happy to buy lots of new dresses.

We were allowed to take only Five Thousand Australian Dollars. However, this limit was not a botheration for me. After disposing everything and counting all the money I would get from my VRS, I still struggled for enough cash. My brother, Abhay Ji, offered to loan me money for the tickets. It was embarrassing for me, but I had no choice. I promised that I would return his loan on priority. It was hard for a family member to extend such help, but Abhay Ji was also my best friend. In the past ten years, I had moved far away from all my relatives, and I was going to leave behind all my friends except one, Abhay Ji.

We vacated the company residence and shifted to the one-room set with Annu. It was the day of my farewell. My engineer friends organised a farewell for me in the executive canteen at 4 pm. Around 10 am, Meghraj Ji, from the Tool Room, approached me and asked me to come to the non-executive canteen at 2 pm.

When I reached there, all the staff, along with Arya Ji and Kulshrestha Ji, were present. They had organised a farewell party for me. It was a pleasant surprise because the Tool Room had not been under my control for the past two years.

"We had very short notice; therefore, we could not do it on a larger scale. We all love you and wanted to bid you fare well. We know you avoid sweets, so we replaced them with cashew nuts." Meghraj Ji was overwhelmed with emotion.

"You people have played a big role in my life. You have helped me in becoming a better person. This will help me for the rest of my life. I acknowledge that I was arrogant, but you all forgave me. You cooperated with me, you loved me, and above all, you remembered me. You all have a special place in my mind and heart." I was emotional. I shook hands with everyone before leaving.

The farewell at the executive canteen was formal. My younger friends were expecting an explosive speech from me. They were waiting to laugh loudly at each of my sentences. They expected the show to be the biggest fun ever, but I disappointed everyone. I was done. My energy had depleted. My throat was dry. My mind had surrendered to my heart. And, my heart was drowning.

"Thank you all for gathering here to bid me farewell. Thank you very much. Thanks." I completed my shortest speech.

Back home, Shalu was shocked to see my drooping face. I had forgotten to remove the flower garland. My face was stoned. My eyes were trying to hold the flood of tears that were threatening to fall. I was speechless. I was robbed. I was left with nothing.

"We will be fine," Shalu consoled me. She removed the flower garland and gently patted my hands.

Shalu's parents, her brother Sharad Ji, and my brother Abhay Ji came to see us off at New Delhi International Airport. We had to stand in a queue for entry. The Security Officer ensured that everyone had a valid ticket and passport. Once you entered through the door, you were not allowed to come out. The only consolation was the glass wall near the door, so we could still see everyone. There was still some time for the check-in process to start. As we waved to everyone who had come to see us off, I suddenly noticed my parents. They had come unplanned at the last moment to see us off.

My dad and mom were waving to us. Mummy Ji was standing on her toes to gain some height and get a better view over the heads of the crowd. I rushed to the gate and requested the Security Officer to let us go out to meet my parents. I wanted to touch their feet and cry like a child and say sorry, but we were not allowed. I could see the fear and anxiety in my parents eyes of departing forever. It was too late. All the pain my parents had taken to rush from Lucknow just to say goodbye had been in vain. How much pain I had given them. How much I undermined their love for me. Had I always been wrong about them still loving me like before? My parents had not left me. I had abandoned them. The thought echoed in my mind: "I will come back to repair the damage."

We were heading towards the check-in counter. I was shaken and confused. Shalu had taken charge and was guiding us. I had lost count of the number of security checks we had gone through. We had never travelled by air, but now we would board an international flight. We were flying with Malaysian Airlines, which was cheaper than Qantas and Singapore Airlines. As we approached our Boarding gate, the sight of the enormous aeroplane filled us with excitement. How could these giants possibly fly?

We boarded the plane. The air hostess approached us with a tray which had lollies and cotton balls. I happily picked some lollies, and so did every one of us. I could not understand the purpose of cotton balls until the plane took off and some passengers pushed them into their ears. As the plane gained height, we all felt the pain in our ears. Ninni and Manu had received their toy bags and were busy exploring them. We took turns at the window seat, though Manu had the lion's share. It was about a six-hour flight to Malayasia, and plenty of food and drinks were served. We were transported to a hotel for the night. The next day, a minibus took us for a local tour. The city was modern and impressive. The Twin Towers were Malaysia's signature. The suburban areas did not look much different than India. We were happy to have visited our first foreign country.

Late at night, we boarded the final flight to Melbourne. This was a much bigger aircraft. It was Manu's birthday and he was overexcited and awake since early morning. A strange feeling of excitement filled my body. We would soon touch the New Land. The country of our dreams. Hopefully, it would provide us with a better and more prosperous life. We would never live in a crisis again. A country of plenty. The lucky country. I was lost in my thoughts when Manu sought my attention. He was looking down from the window.

"Dad, Dad, we are landing at the wrong place." Manu was disappointed.

"Why, what happened?" I asked.

"Look down there. The houses are like huts." Manu explained. I leaned towards the window and looked down.

"It must be a mistake. It seems the aircraft is landing in a nearby country due to an emergency." I agreed with Manu. I was confused and scared. What now? The houses resembled huts due to their pyramid-shaped roofs. The flight captain announced the landing. Why had anyone not told us the reality of Australia?

As we walked out of the airport, Kamarjit was waiting for us. He was accompanied by Paul, an ex-Bharat Electronics employee who graduated from BHUIT. Our family of four and luggage travelled in two cars. He was happy to see us all safe and sound. We were given a room in their house. Kamarjit and his father lived in a three-room unit. This place was a cluster of small units where mostly old couples lived. The units were close to each other. We were advised to be quiet after 8 pm, or the neighbours would complain.

"Get settled. After lunch, I will show you around to help you decide where to seek a place on rent. On Monday, we will go to the bank to open your account, then visit Knox Council to register you for Social Security and Tax File Number." Kamarjit explained the plan of action. Since we had landed in Melbourne on Saturday, we had a couple of days to settle down, spend time with Kamarjit, and learn more about the new country. He informed about our arrival to Sunil, an ex-employee of BE Ghaziabad, who had also migrated some six years ago and was living close by.

Days flew by, and I could not finalise a car or a place to rent. I suffered from sunburn while searching for a house as I had to travel on foot during the weekdays. We were told that Melbourne's sun is harsh and that we must use a cap and a special cream to protect ourselves from the UV radiation. Manu and Ninni were getting uncomfortable being confined to one room. I had to do something before things became ugly.

In the second week, I was able to finalise a property for rent in Clayton. It was about six km from Glen Waverly which was a relatively cheaper area. The house was old and built of weatherboard, so we could get it for $115/week. The house was built on a vast land. This would provide plenty of space for Manu and Ninni to play. The house number was 31, and it was on Manoon Road.

This country seemed to be lucky for Manu. His lucky number is four, as his birthday is on the 4th day of the month. I finalised a car in the same week. It was a Red Toyota Station Wagon for just over $3000. On the weekend, we were going to move to our new place. The Social Security had been approved, and we would get paid fortnightly from the day we had registered. This was a significant relief.

On the weekend, we chucked all the luggage into our car to shift into our new rented place. We were thrilled with our new residence. Kids could play cricket in the backyard. We had no furniture, but the rooms were carpeted, so we could sleep on the floor. There was a wall heater in just one room, but it was a big room. It was the lounge. We all slept in this room as the nights were cold. Our friends suggested that we call the St. Vincent de Paul Society to get some free furniture for the time being. The very next day, they delivered some bedding and mattresses. These were used ones, but they was better than sleeping on the ground.

We were finding it hard to adjust to the new country. Shalu was missing her parents and the extended family. The entire place was extremely quiet. There was hardly any noise from vehicles, human conversations, or birds. The nights were very bright due to the clear sky. It was difficult to sleep soundly in a bright and cold night. Occasionally, we would see a cat in the street. Our friends were busy during the week, so we were all alone.

"You know our priority right now is not about jobs or schools. It is about not going insane. We have to make sure that we maintain our calm and let time take over." I was sitting next to Shalu, holding her hand. I was trying to console her.

"Yes, I know. I am trying, but it is not easy." Shalu replied.

"Maybe we will remember this as the best time. We are together. We will never have much time for each other once I get a job. We do not need to worry about anything. Social Security is enough for the time being, and we can even save some money." I offered a different perspective.

Sunil and Rekha visited us frequently. Both were helpful. Their kids, Nonu, the boy and Annu, the girl, were about the same age as Manu and Ninni. The only issue was that Nonu and Annu did not know Hindi, and Ninni had minimal exposure to English. At home, we always used Hindi as our primary language and continued using it in Melbourne. Once, Ninni shared her confusion with Shalu:

"Mom, Annu is a nice girl, and I like playing with her, but she speaks differently."

"It is just a matter of a few days. You will understand her. She uses a different language." Shalu encouraged her.

Manu started attending a primary school. Ninni went to a family daycare for four hours, three times a week. There was no uniform in the school, and books were provided there. The school bag was meant to carry only a lunch box. This made Manu exceptionally happy. No uniform, no stress of studies, no homework, just play and learn. Ninni was not excited about going to the daycare but she needed to mix with new children, learn a new language, and become somewhat independent.

It had hardly been a month in our new place, and one day, we returned from the nearby shopping centre in Brandon Park. This was our first significant shopping. Our trolly was filled with groceries, utensils, and other utility items which had cost us less than a hundred dollars. I was stacking the non-perishable items in the fridge that we used as cupboard. It was nonfunctional; we had inherited it as part of our rented place. Ninni had just come from the backyard for a temporary break and stood beside me.

I initiated the conversation by saying, "So, Ninni, what do you think? Have I stacked these things correctly?"

"Yup." This was a short and crisp reply by Ninni in a typical Aussie accent. She was in her favourite yellow frock. She was sweating. She stood close to me, very composed, calm, and confident. I turned my face towards her and looked at her momentarily. She had already taken off. How quickly kids adapt to a new environment. They are so agile, flexible, and open. Why can't we adults be like kids? How come we leave behind our best strengths?

I started attending English classes at the AMES Centre (Adult Multicultural Education Services) close to our home. This was about getting some exposure to the new culture and accent. This was a free service and was recommended by Sunil who had exceptional expertise in locating a deal that was hard to beat. Either it would be free or nearly free. He introduced us to garage sales, where people discarded their goods at throw-away prices.

Generally, this was done over the weekends, and you could identify a garage sale by the balloons at the gate. For Sunil, this was an irresistible temptation. He also knew how to save money without compromising the outcome. His financial vision was unbeatable and he was way ahead of us. He had purchased a house with a large land in a prime location and subdivided it. The construction process of the new unit was in progress.

Through Sunil, we came across many more ex-BE Ghaziabad employees. We were invited for lunch on the weekend with one such family. Shalu and I had difficulty reading the Melway, so I always tied up with Sunil and followed him. Today, most cars have satellite navigation, making life simple. About eight families had been invited. It was a gathering of about thirty people, which included kids. The dishes had filled two dining tables. After about three hours, I was exhausted and bored. I invited everyone to my place but cautioned them that there would be fewer dishes. At the most, we would have only four preparations. We left early.

I was applying for jobs but was not getting any interview calls. One day, an ex-BE employee, Rakesh Singh, told me that he might have a job for me. He referred me to a supplier that he worked with. He told me the company was having trouble in maintaining its quality accreditation. He advised me not to mention that I had no formal experience in Quality Assurance. He assured me that with my professional background, I would have no difficulty in dealing with the challenges. BE Ghaziabad had prepared us well. No technical questions were asked in the interview. I was offered the job and was required to start the next day. I had a job within three months of reaching Australia.

My workplace was an SME (Small to Medium Enterprise). It was a metal fabrication shop that was located on the other side of the city. I had to cross West Gate Bridge over the sea to reach my workplace. It would take about forty minutes' drive. The quality audit was only a month away. If the non-conformances were not addressed, then the company would lose its accreditation. The first couple of weeks were difficult. I reviewed the ISO (International Organisation for Standardisation) documents and company quality manual a few times but could not connect the dots. Finally, when I understood the non-conformances, I made minor changes to the quality manual. Auditors were happy to notice that some efforts had been made and extended the grace period by six months.

One of the company's directors wanted me to implement the manufacturing software which they had bought two years ago. I happily accepted the challenge. I could see that this would help strengthen the company's quality system. Both quality and manufacturing systems would go hand in hand. The quality system was mainly a marketing gimmick, but the manufacturing system benefited by streamlining the processes. I had secured my place in the company.

Shalu formed friendships with a few Indian ladies who would pick and drop their children at the same school as Manu attended. Everyone had plenty of time for each other. They were going through similar challenges. Gopal Verma Ji, who was a manager at BE Ghaziabad and used to live close to our house in Ghaziabad, had also migrated to Melbourne with his family. Brij Panwar, a Sunil's classmate from IIT Delhi, had migrated to Melbourne with his family. We, Sunil, Gopal Ji, Brij, and I became family friends. Our kids were of the same age. We would meet almost every weekend. Both Brij and Verma Ji had good jobs and were settled in Glen Waverley.

Diptiman migrated to Melbourne with his family. He was my classmate at secondary college and BHUIT. He stayed with us. His wife, Sharda, was the daughter of my Physics teacher at secondary school. Their daughter Deeksha was the same age as Ninni. It had been about three months since they came to Australia, but he had not yet secured a job. We planned to visit India for three months. I suggested to Diptiman to stay in our home till we returned from India. He agreed. This was a good outcome for both of us.

Shalu had been shopping for our visit to India. This was mainly gifts for our family members. Anything we liked and found helpful was purchased and tagged to ensure that no one was left out. We bought a camcorder. We wanted to capture all the memories. Soon after we migrated to Australia, Suman aunty died in a road accident. We planned to minimise our losses and capture everyone through our camcorder. Our plan was simple. We would stay in Parmesh Sadan at Etah and at Sushila Sadan in Lucknow for one and a half months each. We just wanted to be with our families. Nothing more.

I carried on going for work till the last day. Shalu did a great job with the packing. She did not leave anything to chance. As we boarded the aeroplane, my mind played a trick. I forgot everything about my job, even the names of my colleagues. Memories before migration became alive. Three years of Australia were blocked. The only thing that I knew was India, our motherland. When we landed in India, I did not cry. I do not remember if Shalu did. I was ecstatic. We had made it. Sharad Ji received us. He had hired a taxi from Etah. We headed back to Parmesh Sadan. Ninni was excited to see cows on the road and shouted with amazement, "Animal, Animal". After she did it three or four times, we all started echoing with Ninni, "Animal, Animal".

We had got used to the roads and traffic in Australia and found India very difficult to navigate after so long. Among all this confusion, we reached Parmesh Sadan. Shalu's parents were waiting outside. Manu had already jumped out of the car and joined his grandparents, *Nani* and *Nana*. Shalu was hurrying to get out but dropped something in the car and reached back for it. Ninni held on tightly to me and remained composed.

Munnu Dada was stretching his back. Chunmun and Bhaiya uncle emerged to greet us. The celebration continued. Shalu went inside and scanned each room. Everyone was awake. The Tingals could not wait for morning and joined us. I was unsure who served the tea. The entire atmosphere was filled with joy. Ninni was still sticking to me.

By the next day, everyone had received their gifts. Life had come to a standstill. No one had to go anywhere. It was all about eating, gossiping, and sleeping. We got everyone to agree to have dinners together. Everyone pooled in and arranged for a cook. Evenings were once again filled with festivities. The Tingals and Chunmun always had many stories to share. The ladies were relaxed. Kids could play and dance. I captured a lot of memories with the camcorder.

Before leaving for my home, Sushila Sadan, in Lucknow, I made copies of the video and left it at Parmesh Sadan. Apart from Abhay Ji's family, most of my family was in Lucknow. They all lived close by. I was able to visit them frequently. Once again, there was hardly any activity. Abhay Ji joined us for a week. Three months passed quickly. It was time to go back. We had found our life back in India, though it was short.

I shared with Shalu that it felt like somebody had picked my pocket and I had lost the three years of my life in Melbourne. We boarded the aeroplane for Melbourne via Singapore. We were leaving India again, but strangely, this time I was calm. I was going home. We did not belong to India any more. Melbourne was our home. As our plane landed in Melbourne, I got my memory back. My workplace, colleagues, friends, shopping centres, weather, roads, footpaths, and "Good day" from strangers passing by. As we exited the airport, I was surprised to see our family friend, Mukesh Bhatia. He was smiling.

"This way." He guided us. I was overwhelmed. His station wagon was big enough to accommodate our luggage and the four of us.

21. SHIPWRECK

Soon after we returned from India, Diptiman shifted to his new rented unit. He had found a job. Sunil was pushing us to buy a house. His logic was that I would pay the same instalment for a loan as I was paying as rent. He had taken us to a few houses in prime locations, but Shalu did not like any of them. I could see the benefits of owning a house, but I did not have time. I asked Shalu to look for a house of her choice or go with Sunil's choice. Shalu succeeded in finding a house in Glen Waverley. The house was on a large piece of land. The school was across the road. The bank sanctioned the loan. Sunil and Verma Ji contributed the deposit money, and I sealed the deal. In three months, we would move into our house.

Time flies when you are having fun. We had two distinct friend circles - one from Clayton and the other from Glen Waverley. Occasionally, we would have a combined gathering of the two groups. This was on major festivals like Holi or significant occasions such as birthdays of Manu or Ninni. This was mainly Shalu's initiative. She worked hard and enjoyed the get togethers. Her cooking was unparalleled. Manu was outgoing and a natural leader. Ninni was attractive, pleasing, and welcoming. I was creative and happy to take initiatives due to support from my family. The only catch was that our friends had to tolerate my crude jokes that were often too close to reality and were best left unsaid.

Once, our Glen Waverley friend circle planned to see snow in Melbourne's outer suburbs. By the time everyone agreed with the plan, peak winter was over. We booked a holiday home for three nights. Sunil was our leader. He was the most experienced in Australia and as mentioned, an expert at getting the best deals. Sunil was leading the way. My car was in the middle as I could not read the map. Sir Ji and Brij had to ensure that I was not lost. As Gopal Verma Ji was 12-years senior to me in BE Ghaziabad, I had started calling him Sir Ji. Everyone else adopted this name. By the time we reached our destination, it was dark. Ladies had brought enough food for dinner. This was a remote place.

We could see the first downside of the good deal that Sunil had struck. We were prepared. We had carried kitchen utensils and groceries with us. During dinner, I announced that I would take care of the breakfast every day. Ladies could enjoy a good night's sleep during this holiday. My plan was simple. I had brought a sandwich press that I got in a lucky draw. It was big enough to take a full puff pastry sheet. I planned to use Bubble & Squeak vegetable patties for the stuffing. Two puff pastries and four Bubble & Squeak patties, cooked for just five minutes, would serve four people. Delicious, yet easy and quick. Tara Ji was amazed. No fat, no mess. The kids were happy. It was as tasty as junk food, yet it was filling and seemed healthy.

One day we were sitting on a cliff. After half an hour of searching, we found a patch of ice on a rock. It was hardly four feet in diameter. We photographed it as proof. Sunil and his family had gone further, hoping to find more snow. Little later, Annu, his daughter, came back. She overlooked the ice, stepped over it, and slipped. We all laughed and showed no mercy. Soon, Nonu, his son, and Rekha Ji also slipped. Sunil did the same circus. Amid laughter from everyone, I said:

"This is not fair, Sunil."

"What is that?" Sunil got up and managed to sit next to Rekha Ji.

"Why has only your family enjoyed the snow, though we all have paid equally for this trip?" I asked.

"Shut up, Atul." Rekha Ji interrupted.

For the next three days, we struggled to find anything interesting. Though the kids were having fun as they were happy to be away from home, but Tara Ji was bored. She could not understand what was so great about the place. She could only see a little creek and a narrow fall from the same water.

Back from the trip, we continued visiting each other. Sir Ji had bought a TT Table and squeezed it into the garage. There was not much space left for moving around, yet it was fun. After we finished our game and were enjoying tea, Tara Ji thanked me:

"Bhai Sahab, your cooking was great. Soon after returning

from the trip, I purchased the sandwich maker, and we have been enjoying your recipe almost every day. The kids take it as tiffin as well. It has made my job simple."

"Have you been doing this for the last three months?" I responded in shock.

"Yes, but why are you surprised?" Tara Ji was puzzled.

"Don't you know, these puff pastries and patties are full of fat?" I asked.

"You must be kidding. I always find it difficult to understand you. You always talk in a cryptic language. You make everyone laugh, but I never get it." Obviously, Tara Ji was annoyed. She had been feeding junk food to the entire family for the last three months. All her strict diet had gone in vain. She had to work hard to regain lost ground.

"You are lucky, Tara Ji. You have realised this within three months. I know a family who used puff pastries for two years and gained double the weight." I was not attempting to hide my laughter. Tara Ji blacklisted me. From then on, Tara Ji never believed me.

****

We learned about Hindi and Music classes in a primary school near our house. I was passionate about singing and wanted to find out more. Unfortunately, all the classes were only for children. Deepika Ji was the music teacher. She was exceptionally skilled and gentle. She was a President award winner. She agreed to take Manu and Ninni as her students. I offered her my house to take music classes. She decided to switch over from the next term.

Once the music classes started at our house, I persuaded her to teach me. I was not shy about learning with young kids. Soon, Shalu also joined me in learning vocal music. This continued for about one year. By now, Deepika Ji was well known in Melbourne, and she had many more adult students. She was more comfortable teaching from her home. Kids mostly learned in groups, while adults took individual classes. Shalu and I were taking combined sessions. Every year, Deepika Ji organised a stage performance for all her students. This created a little community of music lovers under Deepika Ji.

It had been a few years since I started learning vocal music. Classical vocal music was challenging, yet somehow my vocal cords were getting trained. I was now able to try Bollywood songs. I had a good collection of karaoke CDs, musical instruments, speakers, mics, and mixers. I encouraged my friends to sing at our regular gatherings at home. None of us could be called a reasonable singer, yet we had lots of fun.

Vipin, who lived six blocks away on the same street as us, was our musician. He enjoyed giving company on the keyboard. In India, he was a professional chef in one of the five-star hotels in New Delhi. Vipin was an all-rounder. He was a good handyman. He could stitch and knit. So far, he had skilfully avoided my request to sing. I had a gut feeling that he could sing, and that day, I was not letting him go. Finally, he yielded and amazed us. Later, Shalu told me that some ten years ago, someone in his family had passed nasty comments about his singing, and since then he had stopped singing. That day, his wife, Manju, cried and shared the story with Shalu. Later, she paid her respects by tying *Rakhi* to my arm, accepting me as her brother.

Once we shifted into our house, Shalu started Family Day Care. The local council regulated this. She was permitted to care for maximum four children up to the age of four years. Parents contacted the council to get care for their young kids during office hours. The council would refer these kids to a Family Day Care, based on availability. This was a good option for us. Shalu could look after Manu and Ninni while also earning some money. After paying the mortgage, essential expenses, and saving for a visit to India every second or third year, there was hardly any surplus left. We painted the house ourselves. Shalu stitched new curtains.

Manu and his friends made full use of the big backyard. They played cricket there. Manu had started learning Karate. This year, we were planning to celebrate Ninni's 10th birthday. We organised a surprise for her. It was a full-size swing with three different attachments. It was installed by a professional just a day before her birthday. Manu and Ninni did not notice it. We had planned a BBQ under the carport in the backyard. All our friends enjoyed the hot food and drinks. Ninni and her friends became busy with the swing. Cajun chicken was a super hit. I had to get more breast fillets from the superstore. Marination took hardly five minutes, and it was ready for BBQ. The party continued from afternoon to late evening.

With time, I took on more responsibilities in the office. With responsibility came more perks, and I had a better salary along with a company car. Shalu was also getting regular income from her Family Day Care. We wanted to buy a brand-new car to reward ourselves for our hard work. The car Shalu drove was not even roadworthy. After visiting a few stores, we settled on Mitsubishi's showroom in Chadstone. We spotted a 2Lt. Lancer. This was unusual. I enquired from the car dealer:

"Why does this car have a 2-litre engine? The Lancer has a 1.6-litre engine."

"This is the latest LS model. Its design is inspired by the sports version. It is a limited-edition model," the dealer replied.

"What do you mean by limited-edition model?" I asked. Manu had already picked up the keywords "Sports, Limited, Latest, 2Lt." He had moved closer to the car and inspected it from all directions. Shalu and Ninni followed Manu. Shalu looked impressed, but Ninni did not have a clue.

"Only a few cars of this model are released. It will stand out from the crowd. Please have a look from the inside." The dealer opened the car door and asked me to take the driver's seat. Shalu jumped into the front seat, and Manu and Ninni took the back seats. Shalu was blissful. Manu was excited and busy scanning every minute detail and feature of the car. I got the message loud and clear. This was it.

The dealer had already secured the sale and was busy upselling. Manu wanted the spoiler. Within half an hour, the dealer had added another two thousand plus to the price. This did not include any insurance cost.

"Your car will be delivered to our store in two weeks. We will take another week to complete it. I will call you next week to update you and give a firm delivery date," the dealer explained.

Manu was disappointed that we had to wait another two weeks or more. He wanted to leave the old car and return home in the new car. On his way back, he wanted to show it to all his friends. After getting back home, I rang the insurance company. After we received the new car, we wanted to sell the old one. Two young overseas Indian students tried to buy it, but Shalu was reluctant. Her conscience did not allow it. What if these young students had an accident? We called the wrecker to pick up the car.

****

We were now looking to buy a bigger house. I got my loan approved, and Shalu took charge of finding a suitable house. We did not want to move far due to the kids schooling. Shalu did not favour a double-storey house, but she accidentally came across such a house which was open for inspection. It was in Wheelers Hill, hardly one-km from our current house, a locality adjacent to Glen Waverley. About five years ago, the owner had done renovation and added a lovely independent living place on the first floor. This included an en-suite bedroom with a walk-in wardrobe and a beautiful family area with a kitchenette. On the ground floor, it had four bedrooms, a lounge, a sunroom, a family area, and a kitchen. The layout of the house looked perfect to Shalu.

The front rooms of the house had large windows to welcome the Sun. It was a corner block, and there was a park on the other side. Effectively, it was open from three sides. Shalu wanted to buy it then and there. The next day, she came again with Manu and Ninni. Manu immediately claimed the first floor. Ninni liked the bedroom that had glow-in-the-dark stars stuck on the wall. This must have been a young kid's room.

"What do you think?" asked the real estate agent. This house had been on the market for about a year, and the agent knew he had a potential buyer. Shalu and Manu could not control their excitement:

"When can my husband inspect the house?" Shalu queried.

"This weekend. I have scheduled another open for inspection from 11 am." The agent replied.

That evening, Shalu gave me the good news. She loved every bit of the house. We had to get it. The price exceeded my approved loan, and I had to confirm with the bank manager. He approved the loan, stipulating that we would need mortgage insurance. I did not understand the implications, so I agreed. On Saturday morning at about 9 am, I received a call from the agent:

"I already have an offer and cannot sell the house to you. It is just a courtesy call. Your wife was interested in this property, so I wanted to inform you." The agent told me.

"How can you do this? You told my wife you had no offer and would wait for us." I was annoyed.

"We can talk, but you must come to my office now." The agent replied.

"Give me fifteen minutes," I responded.

"Why didn't you wait for my offer? What do you want me to do now?" I was sitting in the estate agent's office with Shalu.

"I already have the offer for the price I told your wife the other day. If you give a better offer in writing, I am happy to take it to the landlord now and see if he would consider it," the agent replied.

"I am adding five thousand to the price. Will this do?" I asked.

"That should be fine." The agent replied.

"Please give me the contract." I requested.

"Have you seen the house? Wouldn't you like to see the house before signing the contract?" The agent was cautious.

"It does not matter. I am fine." I insisted.

"Follow me in the car. I will show you the house before you sign the contract." The agent had mellowed down.

We followed the agent. By 9:45 am, we were sitting in our car outside the house. The agent had gone in and came out after about five minutes.

"Give the landlord about ten minutes. Once they leave the house, I will take you in." The agent informed us.

Inspecting the house was just a formality for me, but it

impressed me. The agent told us that this was a single-owner house. These people had built it, and they had been staying there since then. It was clear that the owners had taken good care of it. Recent renovations had increased its charm. The outdoor fish tank and SPA were seductive.

"Could you please make the offer slightly better?" The agent requested.

"How much?" I asked.

"Two grands." The agent replied.

"If this makes the owners happy, it will be my pleasure. At such a deal, it will not impact me much," I said.

The deal was done. We informed our friends and asked them to see the house at 11 am, which was still open for inspection. Bigger loans led to larger monthly repayments. I had calculated and decided to retain and rent the current house. It would be tough, but if we could sustain it for the next three years, we would have our retirement secured. The settlement period was three months. We would shift to our new home in three months and rent out the current house.

Lot of memories were linked with our current house. We could have lived in this house comfortably for the rest of our lives. Our struggle was over. We had three Indian families close by with whom we had developed good friendships. Manu and Ninni were enjoying school. They had to cross the road and jump the fence to enter the school. Both had a good friend circle. Recently, Abhay Ji had visited us at this house and we all had a great time.

The rain made moving to the new house difficult, and we were exhausted. During the shifting, Shalu cried a couple of times. She could not believe how many household items she had collected in the last few years. We had arrived in Australia with just four suitcases, but today, after a full day's hard work, we still could not finish shifting. We slept in the lounge on the carpet. I got up early and was upset.

"Who has turned on the lights?" I wanted to sleep more. No one replied. I looked around. Everyone was still sleeping. The lights were not turned on. We had forgotten to close the curtains. The

Sun had powered the lounge. I was ecstatic. The Sun had graced our house. It took us a couple of weeks to settle down properly. We used the services of Shalu's trainer to dismantle the gym from the old house and assemble it in the garage of this new house. We would park the cars in the court. Manu occupied the first floor. He started enjoying independent living.

Unlike most Indian parents, we did not pressure Manu or Ninni to excel in their studies and become doctors, lawyers, or accountants. We were confident about their capabilities. Both had excellent social skills and were quick learners. Our bottom line was that they become good citizens. At times, Shalu wanted me to help Manu with his studies, but I did not favour it. I wanted him to learn the skills by himself. His VCE score was not the best. He got entry in IT but soon realised this was not the best option. He discontinued higher studies and joined the Army. He was among the first few Indian boys to join the Australian Army.

Manu started his training in Kapuka. Generally, Indian boys are not well-built, unlike their European or Australian counterparts. This was a complete change for him from enjoying absolute freedom to a strict routine. The physical training was challenging and draining. Manu wanted to escape, but this was his last chance to prove himself. We all went to Kapuka for his Passing-Out Parade. It was a proud moment for all of us. It was almost impossible to recognise him at first. His complexion had turned dark. His head was nearly shaved. His facial bones had become prominent, and his cheeks had almost disappeared. The most impressive part was his eyes. They were shining. They were telling us the whole story, "Dad, I have done it." We all hugged him one by one. Ninni had a hero. We stayed there for one night.

Ninni had shifted to the first floor but preferred sleeping in the family area. For some reason, she was scared to sleep alone in the bedroom. She also enjoyed independent living. Whenever friends visited her, we could hear continuous laughter. Deeksha, Diptiman's daughter, was her best friend. Whenever we had a party at our home, all the kids would gather on the first floor, away from any interference from their parents.

Unlike Manu, Ninni was studious. We hardly ever had to give her any instructions. For us, life without Ninni was just not worth it. I would call Ninni by any name, and she would respond. She was an absolute charm. She was a great fan of Michael Jackson. She had a collection of all his songs and videos. She cried like a child at his death. It took her about a whole month to recover from the shock. At times, Ninni complained her poor sleep quality and bad dreams. We consulted our doctor, but she assured us that there was nothing to worry about.

****

Every time we visited India, we found at least one less family member. Soon after we had migrated to Melbourne, Suman aunty died in a road accident. The second visit was for the marriages of Shalu's younger brother, Annu, and her cousin brother, Chunmun. That time, Shalu had gone with Manu and Ninni while I stayed in Melbourne. During the visit, Bhaiya uncle died of a heart attack. By the next visit, Rani Didi was no more. Doctors were unable to make a confirmed diagnosis. She suffered for about eight years. During this time, she kept losing weight until it became unsustainable. Later, Shail Bua died of cancer when we were in India.

If all this was not enough, in 2006, just two days before Shalu's birthday, we got the bad news that Shalu's dad passed away. Shalu rushed to India. Her mother, Saroj, was in shock. She could barely stand without support. Shalu set aside her grief and looked after her mother. We always wanted our parents to visit us in Melbourne. This would not be possible anymore.

Hardly had Shalu's family recovered from this tragedy when her elder brother, Pradeep Ji, and his younger son, Shubham, died in a road accident. Shalu wanted to visit India to see Pradeep Ji when he was in hospital in a critical stage, but I suggested otherwise. I did not want Shalu to live with scary memories for the rest of her life. A few months later, when we visited India, we brought Shalu's mom to Melbourne. Abhay Ji helped us in getting her visa and medical done.

Shalu's mom was frail, both mentally and physically. This was the first time she was travelling by plane, and it was an international flight. She enjoyed the food, movies, and other services provided by the air hostesses. With her headphones on, she was unaware of how loud she was when communicating. Shalu enjoyed this and had no intention of correcting her. She was happy to see her mom excited like a child.

I found it difficult to address her as Mom, so I called her Nani instead. I found affection and informality in this address. All my friends also started calling her Nani. As Shalu was doing Family Day Care, Nani was not alone in the house. She enjoyed the Indian TV channels, which we subscribed to. Once the TV was turned off, she would go spiralling down, remembering her elder son and grandson, who had recently died in a road accident. Both Shalu and I had not much success in helping her overcome her grief, though she was getting better slowly.

She spent a year with us and began to embrace our lifestyle. Ten months passed quickly for Nani. She was now looking much better. She had gained some seven kg. Her confidence was back. Shalu accompanied her back to India. Abhay Ji received them. Sharad Ji joined them the next day. There was a proper ceremony of handing Nani back to Sharad Ji, all safe and sound. Nani's biggest fear was over. She did not want to die in our home in Australia.

Ninni joined university. She had a reasonably good score in VCE and opted for double degree in Fine Arts and Psychology. She was doing well and was experimenting with her creativity. She was focused. She would rather have her friends visit her and have fun at home than go out with them or go to their houses. Continuous laughter from her room was infectious and music to our ears. Her sketching and painting had improved a lot. She had also started experimenting with the Guitar.

Manu was enjoying his army life. He was mostly based in Queensland. The harder he earned the money, the easier he spent it. He purchased our old house some three years back and sold it at a good profit. He had bought a home in Queensland and enjoyed spending surplus money. He worked hard to build his body and was proud to be a soldier. Just when he was about to get married, he broke up. He was brave, but it impacted him a lot. This year, all of us planned to visit India.

Shalu's music teacher from Etah was settled in Ghaziabad. Shalu would always visit her whenever we came to India. She suggested Aishwarya, her distant granddaughter, for Manu. Aishwarya's mom, Sangeeta Ji, was known to Shalu. She had been her senior at Dayal Bagh College in Agra and was now living in Lucknow. Aishwarya had completed her bachelor's in IT and was employed by a reputed software company in South India. This was a good coincidence. My parents were in Lucknow, and we could easily arrange a meeting with them.

Shalu contacted Sangeeta Ji after reaching Lucknow. It was a good catch-up. Shalu knew most of Sangeeta's extended family. Her mom, aunts, and uncles were settled in Etah. Coincidentally, Aishwarya was to visit her parents in Lucknow the next week. A date was fixed to meet them. Manu was reluctant. We suggested that he think of it as a meeting between two old friends, apart from the fact that they have a young daughter and we have a young boy. We promised him that after this meeting, we would not ask him to meet again unless he told us otherwise. Manu agreed.

We reached their residence on time. This was unexpected. Aishwarya's dad, Alkesh Ji, was in the shower. Aishwarya had not returned from shopping. Her younger sister was not at home either. Sangeeta Ji was in a casual dress. She took us to the lounge, requested to be excused, and left us alone. After about ten minutes, she returned with snacks and sweet Gulab Jamuns and then left us again.

Manu was amused and teased Shalu with his facial expressions. He picked up a Gulab Jamun and put it whole in his mouth. It was hot. Most likely, it was heated in the microwave. Just before Manu could take it out of his mouth, a relatively young girl entered the lounge, and Manu painfully managed to keep the sweet in his mouth.

"Hello, how is everyone?" the girl asked. She was holding a shopping bag in her hand. She was dressed casually in jeans and a top.

"We are fine. I am Atul. How are you? What is your name, young girl?" I responded promptly and enthusiastically. As usual, I had no recollection of any names. Even if Shalu had told me all the names before entering the house, and it had been ten minutes since, it was more than enough to clear my cache memory.

"My name is Aishwarya, and I am the elder one." She was certainly annoyed at my casual behaviour. How dare I not even know her name? By now, I should have Googled everything about her and paid due respect. However, I was not embarrassed. No one from my family was ashamed of my behaviour. Instead, everyone laughed as if they were saying, *"Welcome to our family tradition. Formalities have no place here."*

"Well, Aishwarya. Nice to meet you. This is Shalu, my wife. My daughter Ninni, my son Manu, and my nephew Shingu. We are thankful to Shingu for bringing us to this place. I could not have driven in India." I responded with a relaxed smile.

Aishwarya looked at Manu, who was still struggling to swallow the hot sweet but he managed to give her a smile. She was now a little relaxed. So, it was not the other boy, Shingu, who had not even bothered to shave for the last five days and was looking more like a man with a typical Indian belly. Had the proposal been for Shingu, she would have immediately shown us the door. The lioness had backed off for now.

Aishwarya started chatting with us while still standing. In another fifteen minutes, her parents joined us. Nothing special was discussed. We stayed there for an hour or so and then departed. Manu and Aishwarya arranged to meet again to get to know each other better. Aishwarya visited us later and showed her keenness to push this relationship. She knew her parents might resist sending their child to a foreign country.

The marriage was settled, and we organised a little ceremony at my parents' home, Sushila Sadan. Shalu's brothers were keen to join the ceremony and were just waiting for our call. All the functions were to be held on the first floor in the open area under the tent. It was peak winters in India. My parents were not well, so they stayed at the ground level with my uncles and aunties. Aishwarya gave a dance performance on a famous Bollywood song. I joined her, but Manu stayed away. He is a bit shy.

Manu and Aishwarya spent some more time together before Aishwarya returned to join her job. I was not interested in an elaborate marriage ceremony and was keen to organise a court marriage during the same trip. However, this proved impractical. We had to come back for the marriage in less than three months. We made the best use of time and did as many preparations as we could on this trip. I applied for permanent migration for Aishwarya.

Soon after we returned to Melbourne, we had bad news from Parmesh Sadan. Illa uncle passed away. Before we could return to India for Manu's marriage, Raj Aunty, Illa uncle's wife, also passed away, leaving her only daughter, Vrinda, alone. Despite the loss of her parents within three months, Vrinda joined the marriage ceremony.

Before departing to India for the marriage ceremony, we arranged for a reception ceremony for Manu and Aishwarya in Melbourne. Aishwarya's permanent visa was not expected for another six months, so we asked her to arrange a visitor visa. Organising the wedding was incredibly complicated, but we did a reasonably good job. At least, we thought we did. I was happy that my parents could attend the marriage of at least one of their grandkids.

Manu and Aishwarya moved to Brisbane. Less than a year after Manu's marriage, my mother passed away. She had cancer. Shalu and I had visited her earlier and spent some time with her. Naresh uncle, my father's younger brother who lived in Lucknow, had died about six months prior. It seemed like the Goddess of Death had discovered our family's address.

****

A few years later, Abhay Ji and his wife, Ranjana Ji, visited us in Melbourne. It was a welcome change for us. That same year, my sister and her husband stayed with us for about a month, and we truly enjoyed their company. It is always a pleasant change when someone visits from India. We have always encouraged and even promised to sponsor our relatives for visits or to settle them in

Melbourne, but it never materialised. We prepared a list of all the famous destinations and activities to ensure our visitors gain best value for their time and money.

Since Manu had purchased our old house, I had invested in a couple of properties in the Southeast suburbs of Melbourne. Sunil had multiple investment options in this area and benefited from them but the market had changed since, and property prices were almost stagnant in this area. I sold one and focused on developing the other. But later, due to many troubles, and to avoid financial disaster, I sold all the plots that I had built as part of this project.

Ninni was doing well at the university. She had completed her double degree and got admitted into Post-Graduation. She needed a Master's degree, to get a reasonable job in Psychology or to start an independent practice. After finishing her Post Graduate studies, she was tired of studies and wanted to take a break for one year before starting her Master's.

She did casual work for the Psychology faculty. Soon, she had a boyfriend who worked part-time in the same faculty. Ninni wanted to experience independent living. However, we had difficulty in understanding it. Manu had moved out after getting into the Army. Ninni had no job. She had not completed her studies. Her boyfriend had only a part-time job. All this did not make any sense to us. Ninni could see that she would not be able to argue with us.

For the first time, Ninni wanted to follow her inner voice, but she was against a brick wall. One evening, she tried to convince us, but I failed to understand its gravity. The next morning, as she was leaving for the university, we came to see her off. She turned her face towards us and said goodbye. Her face was calm. Her eyes were sad. It was a very different look. For the first time in my life, I felt as if I was looking at a stranger. I could feel the storm approaching, yet I failed to act. That day, late in the evening, Shalu received a call from her.

"I am not coming."

"Where are you? When are you coming? It is already late." Shalu was getting restless.

"I am not coming back," Ninni replied. She hung up the phone.

All efforts to contact her failed. Shalu panicked. She had gone into a guilt mode. I was in the middle of a perfect storm. The harder we tried to reach Ninni, the further she drifted away. None of Ninni's friends gave us her whereabouts. We were unable to get any information about her. The only clue we had was the name of her boyfriend's suburb where she might be living. We searched each street in that locality and recognised her boyfriend's car.

We waited far away in our car to confirm whether she lived there. We caught a glimpse of her. She was alive. For a moment, we were overjoyed. It was our first sight of her after so many months. There was hope. A few days later, we knocked on their door. We bought pizzas from the nearby shop and took Ninni's favourite soft toy, Chota, with us. We were sure Ninni would welcome her Chota, as she had never slept without it in Melbourne. We were wrong. It did not help Ninni either. We had found her hideout. She had to find a new place now.

Somehow, time was passing by slowly. Manu was posted in Wodonga. It is at the border of Victoria, about a five-hour drive from Melbourne. Aishwarya, along with her son Aayan, was staying with us. Aayan was Shalu's lifeline in all adversities. Physical work and mental anxieties were making Shalu hollow. She had become fragile. Despite my best efforts and continuous counselling, she was no more than a living dead.

Whenever she had any spare time, she parked her car far from Ninni's boyfriend's house to get a glimpse of her and returned in despair. I was not even aware of this. On the other hand, Ninni was going through an even more challenging time. She had a breakup and was now living alone. She had found a job, but it was more taxing and paid less. The financial burden was crumbling her.

She wanted to come back, but something was stopping her. Her agony was not yet over. Her nightmares had become worse. Her sleep had become lighter. When it would become unbearable for her, she would drive past our house or sit on our fence in the middle of the night. She did not want to bother us with her problems. It was her journey. This is what she had learned. This is what Manu had learned. This is what I had done. This is what

Shalu had done. We all took pride in our decisions. We all learned from our mistakes. We all pursued our journeys. We all loved each other. We all cared for each other. We all are independent people, yet we all are one.

Aayan, our grandson, was being well looked after by Shalu despite her deteriorating health. He had good company with the other kids in Shalu's Family Day Care. All the kids were mostly of the same age. Aayan was independent, intelligent, and caring. He would keep himself busy without expecting any attention or appreciation. He was learning Hindi and English equally well. He listened keenly to my music practice and developed a good sense of music.

Though he could not speak, he would remind me to make coffee for Shalu, in case I forgot to do so before going to my home office. Before going to bed, he would come to say good night and sweet dreams to us. On his way back, he would ensure that the door was left open by an exact gap. I could not give him much time as I tried to develop new skills to improve my consultancy or employment opportunities. At times, he would amaze us with his communication skills. Unfortunately, he had not met Ninni. She had left us before his birth.

I forgot to mention Rex. Manu had adopted Rex from the RSPCA (Royal Society for the Prevention of Cruelty to Animals) when he was only a few weeks old. It was an American Staffy. It was primarily white with some black patches. When Aishwarya shifted to our place, Rex also came with her. At the time, he was about two years old. He was a quiet and gentle dog. I was against having a pet. I did not like any additional responsibility, but there was more to my learning. I realised that dogs are reasonably intelligent creatures.

Rex treated each family member differently. He would not get on my bed or sofa but would sleep with Manu. He was scared of me, yet he would not let me go alone for a walk and would bring his leash to take him along. Shalu loved him and felt guilty when she had to leave him alone in the house. She would not leave him without giving him a treat and would treat him again after returning. She brought various toys for him and played with him.

Manu visited us every second or third week unless he was on deployment. It seemed he was enjoying the placements. He was averaging more than one assignment every year. Manu, Aishwarya, and Aayan went to India to have a family reunion. Manu planned to take Aayan to Parmesh Sadan and Sushila Sadan to meet his great-grandparents. Unfortunately, my dad died just a few days before Manu reached Lucknow to meet him.

During Aishwarya's stay with us, we felt a bit of a disconnect between Manu and Aishwarya. We did not pay much attention until one of Manu's visits to Melbourne from Wodonga revealed that they were planning to separate. This was shocking news for us. Shalu was worried about Aayan. She had seen many kids from single parents and was aware of the challenges.

There was not much sense in Aishwarya staying with us. Soon, she rented a place and moved to her new house with Aayan. We kept visiting her and Aayan. We were hopeful that this decision was made in haste and was not likely to last long. Aishwarya was going through a reality check and tried to reverse the decision, but not at the cost of her pride. We were supportive of her.

No one should ever compromise on their pride. It is our soul. We cannot sell it cheap. We live by our personalities. We are remembered by our personalities. In the *Gita*, Lord Krishna said, "A Soul is immortal. Air, water, fire, or any weapon cannot destroy it." The soul is none other than our personality. It is our pride. In commercial language, it is our brand. You are born with a body. You work hard to convert it into a soul. The soul that is immortal. The brand that sells.

Gita is a small episode of an epic battle, *Mahabharat*, between the Kauravas and the Pandavas, who were cousins. The Kauravas were a hundred brothers while the Pandavas were five brothers with a common wife, Draupadi. The two families had a rift over the rights of their estate. Lord Krishna, the most influential king of the time, was a distant relative of these families. Lord Krishna offered his help in playing an impartial role in the battle between the two families. They could choose between Lord Krishna's entire army or Lord Krishna himself, who would not actively fight in the battle.

The Pandavas wanted Lord Krishna, and the Kauravas were more than happy to get the whole army. All the Kauravas were killed in the fight, and the Pandavas survived with the guidance of Lord Krishna and their combined commitment towards their wife, Draupadi. I have no doubt that this battle was real, but I have another take. The Pandavas represent the five fundamental substances that are essential for life. They also represent the five senses of our body. Draupadi is a symbol of life and without her, life would not propagate.

The Kauravas represent the unlimited desires of human beings. There is a continuous struggle in our mind between the five basic needs and the hundreds of desires. Deep down, under absolute darkness of our mind, is the delicate control that balances the two. Krishna means dark. Lord Krishna is the darkest part of a human mind that controls the tightrope between the five fundamental needs and hundreds of desires. Gita is the preaching by Lord Krishna to Arjun just before the start of the battle.

After Aishwarya moved to a new place, Ninni got in touch with her. Ninni had bought a Beanie for Aayan before his birth but could not give it to him. She was keen to meet Aayan. She also had a soft spot for Aishwarya. This was excellent news for us. Aishwarya maintained the delicate balance between Ninni and us and provided a much-needed padding so Ninni could return.

Soon, we heard more bad news from Parmesh Sadan. Chunmun died of a heart attack. This was another young death. Chunmun was the joining force within Parmesh Sadan. We all, which included Ninni, had a special place for him in our hearts. Soon after Shalu messaged Ninni about this sad news, she received a call back. Ninni wanted to come to see us. Shalu rushed to tell me this good news. I was working from home due to COVID. Our sorrow was now mixed with excitement.

We plucked flowers from our backyard and came out on the front lawn to receive Ninni. The sound of every approaching car bumped our heartbeats. Ninni came after about 45 minutes. We hugged her. We all cried. Chunmun had done what no one could do. Ninni went back, but she promised that she would keep visiting us. She was back for good.

I picked up a job in an IT company. Within three months, I was able to switch over to another IT company where I could do the job of my choice. However, this proved challenging. The harder I tried, the less I could understand. The environment at the workplace was not helping either. After about ten months, I was made redundant again.

The trash of someone is a treasure for others, which proved true for me, and I got another job within a week. The work environment was great, and the people were helpful, but it did not make the job any easier. I was losing my confidence. My mind could not rest. Shalu's health did not allow her to work full-time anymore. I decided to retire.

We would downsize by selling our house and buying a smaller unit. We would top up our super with the remaining funds. On the day of the auction, we did not get the price which we sought and decided not to sell. This was an act of God. He did not want us to suffer any more losses.

The biggest consolation was that we all had survived. We were still in the same house that had kept us all under the same roof with our good memories. The ship was wrecked entirely, but we all were still alive. There was hope. We could talk again. We could stand again for each other. Together, we could live again.

22. BEYOND AND BOUNDLESS

We were exhausted after the big party that night. I had had a few Beers so was feeling sleepy.

"People enjoy parties at our home. No one wants to leave early. As always, all the dishes were delightful. Everyone thoroughly relished the food and the conversations. Is there too much left over?" I asked Shalu. As she did the dishes, I stood beside her in the kitchen to give her moral support and any little help that she might need.

"No, not much is left. Most people took away the food. I saved some for Ninni. You should not have started the discussion on spirituality. It spreads like a bushfire. Most of the discussion was very bookish. Hardly anyone spoke through experience." Shalu replied, finishing the dishes amazingly fast and stacking them beside the basin. She removed her gloves, washed her hands, and picked up the little towel from the top of the microwave.

"Let us go to sleep. Please turn off the lights and check the gas and heating." Shalu completed her ritual.

"Sure." I double-checked the gas stove and duct heating, turned off the lights, and followed her. Shalu had still not fully overcome her fear of the dark, so I would turn off the lights once she left the family area.

"Have you taken your night pills?" I asked and started snoring even before she could reply. I was comfortable in my first job in Melbourne. When I was kicked out after twenty years, it impacted me deeply, though I did not make it evident to my family and friends. If I had been in the job for two more years, it would not have disrupted my financial plans, but life has its secrets. I could manage my emotions during the day but had no control over my dreams. Tonight, in my dreams, I was returning from the factory where I had worked before being made redundant.

The rain had not completely stopped, even though the Sun had reached a very low angle. This was an ideal condition for the formation of a rainbow. The view of the rainbow from Westgate Bridge was perfect. The rainbow touched the ground on both sides.

It was a double rainbow. Both were rather dark-coloured, as if painted by a kindergarten student. I was captivated by the beauty of nature's miracle. I felt as though I was entering the gates of heaven. Suddenly, my attention was drawn by Ravindra Kumar's distinct voice, who appeared from nowhere. He was in the back middle seat of my car.

"Place this piece of fruit deep in your mouth without biting it." Papa Ji instructed.

I found a big wedge-shaped piece of Guava (Fruit *Amarood*) in my right palm. Confused, dazed, and a bit horrified, I pushed the large piece of fruit into my mouth, but I could not close my mouth. It was very discomforting. I received further requests from Papa Ji.

"Lift your seat. Look far beyond and tell me what you can see."

"Nothing..." I uttered. I was scared.

"Look hard, and then tell me." Papa Ji requested again.

By now, the fruit had melted and made its way into my stomach. The scene through the windscreen was changing. A distant beam of dim light was approaching fast, straight towards me. What could it be? I was perplexed. I could not move my eyes away. The pressure to respond was building up.

"I can see now. I know him. He is Vishwamitra! Followed by Vasistha, Vyas Ji...." One after another, the saints and gurus from the time of Lord Ram and Krishna followed. Everyone was flying past me.

"I can now see great warriors and deities - Arjun, Karn, Surya, Indra ..." I was confused.

"Why are they rushing? Where are they going? Wow!! Hanuman Ji. How muscular he is!" His stretched facial muscles and prominent cheekbones hinted at a monkey-like appearance.

"I have never seen such a muscular person, not even in my imagination. Now I know why people think he is the Monkey God." I paused for a moment.

"Oh, I can see Lord Shiva in a sitting posture. He is absolutely calm and is holding the trident, his favourite three-pronged weapon. Vishnu Ji!" I shouted like a child and continued with the commentary.

"He is in full gear. He has all the weapons: *Gada, Chakra, Dhanush, and Pharsa*. He is wearing a crown. His face is not like a man. He resembles the Hawk. The rays from his face are amazing. He is the supreme power." No one else seemed to be coming now. All of them had disappeared on the other side of the view.

"Papa Ji, where have they gone? Why were all of them together? What was the hurry? How could I recognise all of them by their faces and names? What do I have to do with all this? What was this piece of Guava?" I showered queries on Papa Ji.

Papa Ji had calmed down after listening to the commentary. His face looked content, and his eyes were fixed deep in space. He started speaking softly.

"In Hindi, Guava is called *Amarud*. *Amar* + *Uday*. *Amar* means immortality, and *Uday* means bringing into the light. This fruit brings immortality to lighten up our lives. To see these immortal people, you need to first taste this fruit. It must be something significant that they will discuss, and you must have some important input to offer. That is why they decided to see you on their way." Papa Ji explained.

"What! I have something important to offer! I do not even know what this is all about. I am not an expert on any subject, and these people – Oh, they cannot even be called people. They are Gods. They know everything. They can have anything they want. They are the creators...".

I was stammering and ran out of words. I was aware of how little I knew or could do. My attempts to change anyone at work or in my social circle had failed miserably. I had been working hard to change myself instead of the whole world. Often, many of us find ourselves spending more time justifying our actions rather than taking a moment to analyse them with an open mind. We tend to look outward for answers instead of diving deep within ourselves. It makes one wonder which world holds more significance and complexity: our inner world or the world around us.

"Let us follow them. We need to join them." Papa Ji ordered in a soft tone. Without losing time, both of us glided fast in the same direction, trying to catch up with them.

"When did you come to Australia? Why didn't you tell us about your visit? Even Shalu did not give me the slightest hint." I was puzzled by the gentle smile on his radiant face. I waited for a response. In complete silence, I recalled my last recording session with Papa Ji nearly twenty years ago, during one of my routine visits to India. I felt embarrassed and blushed like a child, realising my mistake. His words echoed in my mind.

"*Soon, I will complete my fifth Yagya of Yoga, after which I will be able to fly and visit any place in the world in no time. You have my promise: I will visit you all in Melbourne. You may not know, but Australia was home to Rishi Atri, so it was called Atrialaya. Atri + Alaya which means place of living or home for Saint Atri. At that time, India and Australia were one island. Later, Australia got separated and drifted far away. The whole Earth looked quite different, with just two main islands.*"

Somewhat recovered from the initial embarrassment, I tried to continue the conversation.

"So, are you still getting along with Krishna Ji? He promised to be your friend, philosopher, and guide, but on the condition that you stop practising as a lawyer. He does not believe in giving anything for free. Doesn't he? I also went through an experience that made me think that sometimes your worst enemies are your best friends. By the way, you still owe me an answer to why Mahabharat is ingrained in my mind. Why do I feel such a strong connection with it? You assured me you would check with Krishna Ji and let me know." I was getting back my confidence.

Papa Ji nodded his face in acknowledgement. We had enjoyed spiritual discussions with each other in the past without having any commonality in our approach. While Papa Ji had a deep-rooted belief and devotion to God through his yoga and meditation, in contrast, I was analytical and practical. I was a science student and an engineer by profession. I do not believe in God in the same way as most people do. I do not deny the existence of a God-like person at any point due to my belief in the theory of probability and normal curves.

For me, the exciting zone on the normal curve is the one that lies outside the six-sigma region. Both idiots and Gods reside on opposite sides beyond the usual Six Sigma region that encompasses 99.99966%. Simply put, 1 in 3,000 people possess great talent, 1 in a million exhibit extraordinary talent, and 1 in a billion surpass our imagination. This also gives me an explanation of multiple Gods and a hierarchy among them.

"So, who would you like to see first?" Papa Ji asked very humbly as I struggled to maintain pace with him.

"Can I see Hanuman Ji." I responded. I was lagging and was amazed at Papa Ji's fitness. How could a 78-year-old person of average height, weighing less than 42 kg, possibly beat me? I was looking forward to my Black Belt grading in karate soon.

"He might give me the secret of your vitality and agility so that I can keep pace with you. Apart from that, I have little complaint to make. What fun would it be to get a few tips from the pinnacle of martial arts. I can also verify your version of the story of Ramayan which we had recorded back in 2004." I quickly offered my justification. After a little pause, I continued in a serious tone.

"Sometimes it is in the best interest of the overall society to let victory go and accept defeat. Ravan may be one of those exceptions, who deliberately embraced humiliation of defeat before touching the final destiny of death." I sympathised with Ravan. The story of Ramayan by Papa Ji flashed through my mind. My face turned grim. I stopped gliding and looked towards Papa Ji, who was surprised by my sudden halt. He had never seen me with such a serious expression and wondered what was going through my mind. There was complete silence until I started speaking slowly but firmly.

"I wonder why sometimes people struggle to think clearly." I paused.

"If Kaikeyi had really hoped that Bharat would become the king of Ayodhya, it makes me wonder why she had not brought it up with Dashrath before. It is always a good idea to clarify our thoughts and not assume that things will just fall into place. When we are looking for a favour in return, it is important to clearly express our needs and communicate openly, especially when there is no crisis at hand. It does not help to raise an alarm once the situation has already gone out of hand. Family means openness, understanding, and unconditional love." I returned to the present time.

"Why do parents try to shape their kids' futures instead of supporting them in discovering their own? Kaikeyi never asked her son Bharat about his wishes to be a king; she simply made that choice for him. It can be tough to figure out what we want to accomplish in life, and yet we find ourselves advising others and feeling frustrated when they do not take our guidance as gospel." I was trying to fit the pieces of the puzzle.

"If Srupnakha was confused by Ram's objections to her marriage with Lakshman, I wonder why she did not clarify with him. Perhaps it could have been as straightforward as Lakshman was already married or just much younger than her. By having an open conversation with Ram, she would have had the opportunity to take charge of her destiny. Imagine how impressive it would have been for her to show Ram her boldness, openness, and eagerness to work through the issues instead of letting them get complicated! After all, isn't it essential to have such qualities if you aspire to be part of a royal family or even a respected family?" I continued with my doubts.

"How could someone as remarkable as Ravan let himself be led astray by fate? What truly counts is the journey we embark on, rather than just the destination. Even if it was true that his daughter might bring about the end of his lineage, it certainly does not justify his choice to harm or abandon her. Perhaps she could have been the key to realising his dreams and elevating his dynasty to a level where legacy and love would outweigh mere survival." My questions had no end.

"Did Ravan pay a high price for creating a secret within the family? One should not keep secrets in a family. Ravan's sister discovered his secret and then exploited him. Family means trust, not fear. Everyone makes mistakes, and this is how we learn. Then why should we hide our hard-earned lessons from our loved ones?" I was struggling to contain my emotions when a deep voice boomed:

"So, you have a grudge with me, son."

My heart stopped for a few seconds, and my whole body froze. I felt like I was standing in front of a truck on a highway with its high beam on. When my retina muscles were squeezed to their limits, I saw two people, twice my size, extremely well-built, standing before me. God, Hanuman Ji was looking straight towards me. The excessive blood flow had turned the colour of his body to almost red. It was just impossible to make any sense of his expressions due to his stretched facial muscles. Standing next to him was Bheem, somewhat normal looking and with an encouraging smile on his face.

"Tail…" As if the cork of a shaken sparkling wine bottle had blown away. Words were automatically coming out of my mouth.

"I was just kidding. Oh God, I always wondered why everyone worships you. Is it because you crossed the sea once? I cross the sea, I mean, I travel through Westgate Bridge every day. I am really sorry, Sir. I did not mean it at all. Honestly, I was kidding. I never meant to compare...". My voice choked. A burst of crackling laughter like thunder filled the air. This was Bheem.

"You think he has a tail." Bheem lifted me with one hand. He was laughing hysterically. He took me behind Hanuman Ji and continued:

"**So where is his tail? Did not Papa Ji tell you what this is all about? Anything else you have for him? Let him go; he has a lot to do, but I like your sense of humour. I will give you a tip. Let your fear kill your enemies, not yourself. Living in fear kills a live person; death is a blessing."**

Bheem finished speaking, and then both Bheem and Hanuman Ji disappeared in a fraction of a second. I could see Papa Ji vanishing in the same direction. I was left alone, shaken, and frozen. My dream was over. I was awake but confused. The dream was so vivid that it was hard to accept it as unreal. I was searching for my existence. There she was. Shalu was in a deep sleep next to me. I touched her to make sure it was all real.

I was overwhelmed by the experience. My mind went blank as if nothing was left to think about. I had reached a point that was Beyond and Boundless—beyond the real world and free of any restrictions. Slowly, the thoughts started flowing again.

We have come across many stories, both grand and humble. I wonder if it is just about reading them or discovering our own roles within these tales, like the Ramayan and Mahabharat. Throughout our lives, these timeless tales continue to unfold in various forms. It helps us to reflect on the characters that we embody to achieve the desired outcomes. Are we stepping into the shoes of Ram, Ravan, Kumbh, Vibhishan, Sita, or Srupnakha? If so, what kind of future are we envisioning? How are we guiding our society? Are we ignoring Draupadi's insult? Or, even worse, are we fostering an environment where Draupadi is forced to strip her clothes in public? If the insult of one woman has the power to dismantle the pride and integrity of all men, then how much longer can we sustain this existence?

I have come to realise that honesty in relationships is absolutely essential. Before we connect with others, it is important to first build a strong connection with ourselves. We should always strive to be honest with ourselves. Our responses need to reflect who we truly are rather than what we think we should be or what others expect us to be. While often discussed, love can be the most misunderstood concept. Countless stories and movies have explored it, and so many people have fought battles and even lost their lives in the name of love. Nowadays, many marriages or partnerships are formed primarily on the foundation of love between two individuals, free from the influences of family or friends. So, why don't we see more stability in these relationships? Why do some people choose to live alone? Why are families delaying or even opting out of having children? The underlying issues are often more complex than they appear.

In many long-term marriages, especially within Indian society, after retirement, men feel out of place in their own homes. It seems that, upon finishing their professional journey, they also lose the respect of their wives. They struggle to pick up household skills like cooking, cleaning, and laundry. Wives feel that their husbands' presence the whole day intrudes upon their space. Previously they took pride in caring for them, but now the wives expect them to share the household responsibilities, even if they are not trained to do so.

True partnership means not keeping our cards close to our chest but sharing them openly with our partners. Can we help our partners in becoming independent and strive to make them better people every day? Can we encourage them to embrace positive changes and guide them in letting go of bad habits? Maybe by building a healthier family unit and nurturing strong, well-rounded children, we can contribute to society at large because a family is the very foundation of a society, and every individual has a role to play in that foundation.

Love is not just something we discover one day; it is something we nurture and grow together. Just like any beautiful plant, it needs the right soil and the right environment to flourish, and yes, it does take time. At its core, love is all about caring. To truly care for someone, we need to have empathy in our hearts. When two people care for each other, it naturally fosters mutual respect that blossoms into love. Once that love begins to take root, we forget the struggles and efforts it took to create that rich soil of care and respect. Effortlessly and joyously, love and respect become a part of us.

We must cherish and protect the tender little sprouts of love from the challenges that arise around them. Love grows slowly and delicately, but once it matures, it rewards us abundantly with the care and respect that nurtured it. Care is not always reciprocated in the same way. For instance, when a mother cares for her baby, it is returned in the form of encouragement by moving every little muscle: hands, legs, fingers, belly, cheeks, eyes, mouth, and heart. We all rely on the care of others because care is not a one-way street; it needs to flow back and forth in various forms, whether physical, psychological, or emotional.

I must admit that life is not simple for most of us. Everyone has a tale to tell and experience peaks and valleys. It is an individual journey, but a companion makes a whole lot of difference.

I have found my love in Shalu, and she has found love in me. We have two lovely offsprings, Manu and Ninni. We have built our Parmesh Sadan, where we all live in our most natural way. No one pretends. No one hides anything. No one fears saying anything. Yet, we have respect for each other. Yet there is love among each other. Where are you on your journey to Parmesh Sadan? Are you living in Parmesh Sadan? Have you started building your Parmesh Sadan? Or, are you planning to build your Parmesh Sadan? It is a journey. It is a challenging journey, but it is worth it. Our best wishes are with you.